Praise for Shift

Whether you are a People and Culture geek or just a passionate leader, *Shift* provides the perfect playbook to shift organisational culture. Meredith's extensive firsthand experience guides you through every step, including reflections and experiments to help achieve real change. This book combines the essential ingredients of great storytelling, practical tips and a touch of theory in a great how-to guide for cultural change. I recommend it to anyone who genuinely wants to improve their culture and build a great organisation.

Michelle Williams
Chief People Officer, The Lottery Corporation

Culture matters. In *Shift*, Meredith explains culture in a clear, actionable way to help leaders understand its importance and provides practical concepts to build and sustain a great workplace culture. If you are unsure where to start or feeling a bit lost, I highly recommend *Shift* as the perfect guidebook and companion to help you on your culture journey.

Neil Singleton
Insurance Commissioner, Motor Accident Insurance Commission

Meredith has written a truly practical guide to culture. A handbook full of thought-provoking dimensions of culture connected to real-life data points and experiences. I love the GRASS framework, which provides a way to force oneself into considering the total cultural landscape. My favourite quote is, 'Rituals enrich and reinforce cultures'. What a great way to think about everyday events that affect people's views of culture.

Andrew Matuszczak
Non-Executive Director and Group Executive

Meredith Wilson pushes through where other culture books stop. At the point of providing tips for actions leaders could take, she shifts gears into building momentum, creating a flywheel for culture wrangling that allows organisations to harness their uniqueness.

Callum McKirdy

Author, Coach & Advocate, Different Thinking

'Culture is your day job.' This is one of many straight-talking and high-impact gems from Meredith's book. Finally, someone has written a book on culture that cuts through the jargon and applies to organisations big and small. Every leader should read this book and apply its wisdom pronto.

Belinda Brosnan

Executive Coach, Author & Leadership Change Agent

I wish I'd had access to this book at the outset of my leadership journey. Nonetheless, *Shift* is equally valuable at any career stage as it's insightful, engaging and so practical. I loved the real-world exemplars drawn from Meredith's depth of experience across multiple industries and the immediately implementable tools to shift culture as an organisational leader. This book is a leadership gift and a joy to read.

Elizabeth Eakin

Senior Academic Leader, The University of Queensland

Few people have studied organisational culture as exhaustively as Meredith Wilson. If you're leading change, transformation, a movement or a revolution, *Shift* should be required reading.

Dan Gregory

Co-Founder, The Behaviour Report

Meredith is an outstanding leader on culture, and this book does not disappoint. There are so many takeaways to shift gears and shape culture wherever you are on your culture journey. Meredith's thinking is contemporary and refreshing, supported by practical and enabling culture change opportunities to experiment with. Take the OAR now!

Debra Briscoe

Board Member and People & Culture Executive

Prepare an ample supply of sticky index tabs because you'll need plenty to capture the remarkable insights that Meredith imparts about organisational culture. Her wisdom will undoubtedly provide valuable guidance for you to 'shift gears' and 'lead a culture worth belonging to'.

Kerith Culley

Strategic People Leader, Culture Shifter, and General Manager Operations,
Churches of Christ in Queensland

Many business books on big business topics like leadership, culture, productivity and performance talk about shifting mindsets, states or strategies. But those that resonate the most for me talk, simply and elegantly, to shifting behaviours. Meredith Wilson's book *Shift* has that beautiful simplicity and elegance. She offers lots of practical things that you and your team can do to shift your culture in the right direction.

Dermot Crowley

Author of Smart Work, Smart Teams and Lead Smart

This book has the unique feel of a coaching session with a leadership coach; it's a practical, actionable, enjoyable conversation. *Shift* helps make culture tangible for leaders and provides a blueprint to leverage everyday actions for impact. In a competitive talent market, it is a must-read for leaders wanting to create a competitive advantage through culture.

Andrea McDonald
Director, u&u. Recruitment Partners

This book is modern, meaning it's relevant to the way we work in 2023. *Shift* is full of references, quotes and examples reflective of today—not old school. We are seeing a shift in how we treat our people and this book gives some great tips and insights. This book is not just about talking; it's about doing.

Michelle Bowditch
Founder, Door20a + Australian Assembly of Administrators

Shift is such a relevant book for right now. Things need to change; organisations need to update how they operate and treat their people and ensure that their culture is fit for the future of work. It can be complicated. If they choose to do nothing, it's at their peril. Good people are drawn to great cultures. I love how Meredith demystifies culture and breaks it down for us. 'Cultures are caught, not taught.' Absolutely! Do you think you have a cultural issue? Do you have a hunch you want to test out? This is the book to help you figure that out.

Emma McQueen
Business Coach and Mentor

Short, easy to follow and packed with 'Oh-Yeah' moments. Meredith shares practical, achievable, real-life examples of how we can all help shift and grow a positive culture in our workplace. Whether you are in a team or leading it, this is inspirational reading. I challenge you not to find something within that you can act on or adopt right now! This book is full of great ideas for growing a resilient, effective and fun workplace. I'm certain that, like a map, it will guide you as you navigate the culture challenges ahead. *Shift* is one 'moment that matters'. I promise you will be inspired to pick up the OAR and play your part in creating a work culture your whole team can be proud of.

David Galloway OAM

Leadership Coach and Facilitator, The People Game.

Shift is an insightful, thought-provoking, and highly practical guide to all things culture. Meredith's use of real examples and stories throughout the book makes the lessons relatable and engaging for everyone. In the context of rapidly changing expectations of corporate culture, *Shift* is a must-read for all leaders, at all levels, in every organisation. Applying (even just a few) key principles will help you create meaningful and positive change in the moments that matter. I can't recommend *Shift* more highly!

Karlie Webster

Managing Director, The Culture & Leadership Collective

Too many books on culture serve too much Kool-Aid to be practical and useful. In *Shift,* Meredith provides leaders (and everyone else!) with real, useful and important actions and models to undertake. My teams and I have benefitted from the wisdom within, and you can too. Feel the GRASS. Take up the OAR. Make culture actionable.

Dave French

Management Consulting Principal Director, Accenture

Shift is a powerful guide to nurturing the greenhouse of culture. Utilising storytelling and personal examples, Meredith provides a pathway for leaders to shape a sustainable culture that is enduring and transformational.

Grace Westdorp

Executive General Manager—Health, Safety & Sustainability, InvoCare

The work environment people want is choice, connection and contribution. They want culture! *Shift* is all about culture, which is easy to say and very challenging to control. Meredith breaks the complex into simple actions. She makes something that seems impossible, reachable. I love how Meredith makes it clear that culture is everyone's job. For me, the perception that you can delegate culture is concerning, and as Meredith puts it, 'the rebranding of HR to People and Culture has not helped this'. Culture is every action, every day, by everyone.

Louise Ferris
Chief People Officer, McCullough Robertson

Shift was a pleasure to read. Meredith's humour and wealth of experience kept the book engaging from beginning to end. The elements of 'on purpose, with purpose' resonated throughout the GRASS model chapters, inspiring all leaders to take action. The Experiment and Reflection sections help apply theory in practice and make a great reference point for future check-ins.

Chloe Stewart-Tyson
Director, Workplace Transformation & Wellbeing, Beca

In the realm of small business, I used to regard 'culture' as a vague term from university textbooks. However, Meredith has expertly explained its significance and how we can practically effect change. The intangible has become tangible, allowing us to foster a truly enjoyable workplace culture. If you aspire to make a genuine impact on your organisation and the world, a great starting point is to read *Shift* and implement the changes your organisation deserves and the world needs.

Gary Brown
Chief Hatcher, Hatcher Advisory

Meredith's experience and passion for her work certainly shine through in this book. It provides unique ways to understand and describe culture—what it is and what you want it to be, together with practical, thoughtful, and purposeful ways to go about culture shift. This is not a book to read once and put on the bookshelf, it will stay on my desk and be used to reflect when needed.

Lea Slade
Senior Director, Health & Safety, Newmont Corporation

They say the soft stuff is the hard stuff, and getting the soft stuff right is not easy, even for experienced executives. Like Meredith, I am fascinated with organisational culture and have explored many ways to move the culture of the places where I have worked. Meredith's book is a wonderful summary of work on culture to date, and she provides a nice way for leaders to consider shifting the culture with her GRASS model. This is 'culture by design' in action. I love it and will use it to help guide my next piece of work on culture.

Andrew Steele
RE-THINK HR

Shift is a remarkable and empowering book that highlights the transformative power of culture. It offers practical strategies and profound insights, making it an indispensable resource for both personal and professional growth.

Melissa Crossman
CEO, Cryptoloc Data Security

Meredith's book is a generous gift to OD practitioners and leaders on how to practically shift culture, one experiment at a time. It's an expansive collation of real-life ideas gathered from decades of coaching individual leaders and executive teams through transformational change. We should all challenge ourselves to assess our current organisation cultures in terms of what should be retained, refreshed or replaced, what is required and what we can 'reach' for. You'll thoroughly enjoy reading *Shift* and the opportunity to soak up Meredith's wisdom.

Tanya Day
People & OD Leader, Nous Group

Meredith Wilson's engaging book *Shift* is full of tangible and relatable examples of her Cultureshift formula at work. I particularly love her explanations of 'moments that matter', so simply explainable (and easy to remember) as GRASS. Meredith takes us through these tools and strategies, some we might already use and some new ones for our kitbag. Crucially, she urges us to look at shifting culture as a deliberate and ongoing process. *Shift* is a perfect roadmap in the important job of leading culturally positive, productive and safe organisations.

Katherine Hoepper
Arts Executive & Leader, The Little Red Company

With a wealth of experience and expertise, Meredith Wilson constructs a compelling case for the profound impact of investing in your culture, not only in business but also on a deeply human level. A mandatory read for leaders in every sector; *Shift* will inspire introspection, reflection, and transformative action. Open your mind, open your heart, and allow this exceptional book to empower you towards a future defined by purpose and lasting impact. The truth within these pages will guide you towards becoming an extraordinary leader—one who understands the immense power of culture.

Monique Richardson
Service Leadership & Customer Service Expert

For years I've heard that culture is confusing and too time consuming for investment. Meredith's book *Shift* provides an understanding of culture without boxing it to one definition. I love the practical elements that will make the difference for any executive, leader or team.

Lana Johnston

Executive Coach, Board Director and Advisor

Shift is jam-packed with incredibly practical wisdom. Meredith makes the application and transformation of culture that has eluded so many for so long, really doable in the day-to-day. Suited to organisations of all sizes, you will come away with the tools and inspiration to create an eminently catchable culture. Once applied, the lessons will positively shape your leadership and your organisation. *Shift* is hard to put down and is a must-have in your business library.

Chris Green

Author, Mentor, Strategist, Facilitator

Practical, engaging and, above all, inspirational. Wilson's knowledge, experience and passion shine through in *Shift*. She provides a simple formula for cultural change with clear explanations and plenty of examples on how to put them into practice. Every leader on the planet will benefit from reading this book.

Bryan Whitefield

Director, Bryan Whitefield Consulting

I love this book! It gives people an insight into culture, which is often perceived as ambiguous and complex. Meredith explains it in a way that is relatable, with practical ways to make positive change. I wholeheartedly agree that we should be creating a positive culture because it's the right environment for our people to thrive, although it's great that Meredith makes the connection between culture and improved business performance. Starting today, I'm looking through the lens of GRASS!

Maree Dalzotto

Head of HR Business Partnering, WSP Australia

Do yourself and your company a favour and pick up this book. Wilson distils years of experience and lessons from the highest echelons of corporate Australia into the core principles of what makes a great organisational culture and how you can help to shape one.

Alex Hagan

Futurist & Author

I have worked with Meredith Wilson for many years. Her knowledge of culture and the link between culture and leadership is both leading edge and practical. In recent years I have specialised in supporting boards by identifying shadow cultures and their link to aberrant behaviour. Meredith's book, *Shift*, introduces simple actions leaders can take to address the most common causes of these kinds of destructive cultures.

Ian Doyle

Board Advisor, Effective Governance

Whether you are an emerging leader or a seasoned CEO, *Shift* is required reading. It will challenge you to re-think your understanding of culture and stimulate you to reconsider how you lead for cultural change. Meredith has written all this in a style that is conversational and easy to digest. I read this book in a time of cultural turmoil. It has given me the perspective to review, assess and ponder. Importantly, *Shift* has given signposts to the answers to my questions and the creative thinking about how to make positive change.

Andrew Farr

Workplace Law Partner, PwC

I loved every minute of *Shift*. I found myself smiling, laughing out loud and shaking my head in agreeance. (Although I'm not sure what the passengers on my flight thought.) My highlighter was out and I was busy noting so many valuable insights that I will be able to bring into my business. Thank you so much for your honesty and your pragmatic tips and suggestions. *Shift* is a must-read for all leaders on the true meaning of culture.

Tash Macknish
Group Manager, Organisational Development & HR, Data#3

If you're the kind of person who appreciates that business is personal, then *Shift* is for you. Meredith has drawn on her wealth of professional and personal experience to create a veritable playbook for culture crafting. I have worked with Meredith in a variety of roles over the last 15 years and can confidently say that she knows what she's talking about. This material is as relevant for team leaders and project managers as it is for small business owners and senior executives.

Michael Derwin
Project Delivery Specialist

If you are searching for an evidence-based, trustworthy source of information, this book is for you. Meredith's presentation of complex concepts in a practical and easily digested format makes this book useful to executives, managers and team members alike. She is a sage for all things culture!

Gaenor Walker
General Manager, National Injury Insurance Scheme Qld

Shift

Shift

Everyday actions leaders
can take to shift culture

Meredith Wilson

Published by Meredith Wilson

First published in 2023 in Brisbane, Australia

Copyright © Meredith Wilson

www.meredithwilson.com.au

Edited by Jenny Magee

Typeset and printed in Australia by BookPOD

ISBN: 978-0-6458667-0-4 (paperback)
eISBN: 978-0-6458667-1-1 (ebook)

A catalogue record for this book is available from the National Library of Australia

Dedication

This book is dedicated to all the leaders
I've worked with to shift culture.

This book is for you if you find books
about culture too stuffy or too fluffy.

This book is for you if you think shifting
culture is hard and big and not for you.

This book is for you if you think shifting
culture can only be done through
organisation-wide initiatives.

This book is for you if you think
culture is someone else's job.

This book is for you if you think culture work can
only be done by people in shiny suits (experts
or consultants from outside your organisation).

This book is for you if you just want to
get on with shifting your culture.

This book is for you if you want
a culture that works.

Contents

Part 1

Culture Matters

The Story Behind Culture Matters

I've always loved culture. My siblings and I were raised with wanderlust. My father travelled around the globe for work, returning home with gifts for us from places far away. Some were consumable (hello Swiss and Belgian chocolate). Electronic games and toys came from Japan and Korea, none of which survived our attention. Many of those souvenirs are still on my cabinet shelves, mixed now with my own collection of travel keepsakes.

My interest in the cultures of different countries and regions drew me to travel widely in my twenties. I studied economics, history and languages at university because I wanted to be a diplomat. I imagined being paid to explore the world, so I sought out psychology, linguistics, sociology and anthropology. I was fascinated by how people interact, why they behave the way they do and the decisions they make. Behavioural economics and systems thinking remain key to how I understand the world today.

I became particularly intrigued by the influence leaders could have on nations and the behaviour of their followers. That fascination remains. Most of my formal post-graduate learning has focused on organisational culture, leadership and behaviour. Yet most of what I have learned and shared in the following pages comes from my experience leading teams, growing leaders, and shaping, shifting and sustaining cultures in organisations across a variety of industries and parts of the world. My experience of cultures that work.

Over the 25 years that I have worked in, on and around culture and leadership, what has struck me is that while nearly all leaders believe culture is important, too few feel confident and competent to change it. Many think of culture change only as a big organisation-wide thing, separate from their everyday.

Yes, culture is complex and intangible, but it is also observable and actionable. Culture is intangible, but its performance impact is not. By understanding culture, and the actions you can take to shape and shift it, you will achieve results through culture.

Yes, culture is organisation-wide, but it is also local. As a leader, your everyday actions contribute to the broader culture and determine the culture of your team.

I am passionate about simplifying culture and making it actionable for leaders so they feel confident and competent to shift their culture every day, and not rely on experts to do it for (or to) them.

This book has three parts. The three parts nest like the Babushka dolls my father bought back from his trips through Russia and Eastern Europe. Each part will shift gears.

Part One focuses on understanding culture, why culture matters, and busts some myths to make culture simple and actionable. This lays the groundwork for you to learn how to shift culture.

Part Two shifts to actioning culture. Here I walk you through my GRASS model, digging into five areas where you can take daily action to shift your culture. With experiments and questions to challenge your thinking, here is where you learn how to 'do' culture, everyday.

Part Three shifts you into momentum outlining how to hit the ground running, and win both the sprint and the marathon that is the work and art of shifting culture.

I've written this book so you can read from start to finish, a chapter at a time, or dip in and out, go deeper on certain topics, pause, skip forward and come back later.

Leaders, may it inspire you to shift your culture every day.

1

Culture Matters Now More Than Ever

If you're like many of the leaders I work with, you want to work on your culture but don't know where to start. This book is for you.

The challenge for leaders

Most leaders believe culture impacts performance. Fewer leaders feel confident they know how to shift culture.

We know what culture is.

The term 'culture' is now so widely used that we all understand it fairly well. We could probably define it broadly and describe the culture we work in at a high level. Most of us know that culture is more than beanbags and ping-pong tables. Yet we struggle to go deeper than high-level definitions like 'it's the way we do things around here' or beyond surface descriptions like we have a 'safety culture' or a 'culture of innovation'.

We know culture is complex.

Most media articles talk about 'good' or 'bad' culture. The media might describe a culture of bullying, but it takes more than a simple assessment to shift it. We know culture is more than a single element, but we are challenged to identify them all.

We know culture is important.

From successful football clubs to classroom culture, culture matters. Sixty-seven per cent of respondents in PwC's 2021 Global Culture Survey[1] considered culture more critical for success than strategy or operating model, and 81% attributed culture as a point of competitive advantage. While there are still non-believers out there, they probably aren't reading this book. You are. That means you value culture enough to want to learn more.

We know culture can be changed on purpose.

PwC's survey found that a staggering 80% of team members are disappointed with their organisation's culture, 76% of leaders believe culture is changeable, and 65% of leaders believe they need to change their current culture.[2] Yet only 15% of organisations report culture transformation programs as successful.[3]

So, if we believe that culture is important and can be changed, why is it so hard?

Culture matters

Leaders both over- and under-estimate the value of culture. They tend to over-estimate the health of their organisation's culture, how well they know the culture and the organisation's capacity to change. Leaders tend to underestimate culture's influence on strategy, execution and transformation efforts. The potential of culture remains untapped in many organisations and a barrier in many more.

Culture has always mattered. It has been a differentiator for great organisations. The company SC Johnson produces household and cleaning products with brands recognised throughout the world. It is family owned and currently

Leaders both over- and under- estimate the value of culture.

has a fifth-generation Johnson at the helm. In 1927, at its annual Christmas party, CEO Herbert Fisk Johnson Snr announced a range of employee benefits that were unusual for the times. These included a 40-hour working week, a profit-sharing plan, and a pension plan. He said, 'The goodwill of the people is the only enduring thing in any business'.[4]

Long before Richard Branson made it famous, JW Marriott's Washington DC root beer stall in the 1920s had the motto, 'Take care of your people and they will take care of your customers'.[5] This maxim is core to Marriott International's culture today. In Sir Ove Arup's key speech delivered in July 1970, he described his ideal of a humane organisation as 'human and friendly despite being large and efficient. Where every member is treated not only as a link in a chain of command, or as a wheel in a bureaucratic machine, but as a human being whose happiness is the concern of all.'[6]

American author Jim Collins' decades of research, described in his books *Good to Great, Built to Last, How the Mighty Fall* and *Beyond Entrepreneurship 2.0*, identified common threads through great organisations with years of success: leadership and culture.

Cultures that work

No culture is perfect, but some are better. Some cultures work for you and some work against you. Your expectations of what a good or great culture looks and feels like will be influenced by what you have been exposed to. It's certainly easier to identify a toxic or bad culture. If you're not sure, here's what I look for.

> You know a culture is good when it works.

You know a culture is good when it works. That is, a culture that enables positive, productive work.

You know a culture is working when people feel they belong and can bring their best.

You know a culture is working when the collective effort is stronger than the sum of the parts. A good culture is where people feel safe and hopeful for the future.

You know a culture is working when people are clear on and feel connected to the organisation's purpose, where individuals and teams can learn, fail, grow, and develop mastery. Cultures that work enable and accelerate change efforts.

You know a culture is working when people have genuine choices and work autonomously toward shared goals. Too often, a great place to work is judged by the perks, treats and trinkets on offer. Cultures that work don't require free food and rock-climbing walls. Cultures that work, work even when systems don't. Good cultures find great workarounds for the right things. Cultures that work make work worth doing.

Cultures that work against you

You know a culture is broken if good people don't care or leave. They likely leave because they are bored, disenfranchised or disengaged. It's even worse when they stay; captives are contagious. You'll end up with more bored, disenfranchised and disengaged team members. You know a culture is working against you when you spend your time and energy on the wrong things. And when you spend more time doing business with yourselves than with your customers. Political environments where you have to spend more time smoothing the way than doing the work. A culture where power and status are misaligned with accountability, or you have to manage up to be successful. Or perhaps bureaucracy is getting in the way in a culture where process and policy matter more than pragmatism and outcomes.

Cultures that don't work frustrate and slow change efforts. They can't be fixed with free food and rock-climbing walls. Cultures that don't work won't work even when systems are good. Broken cultures use workarounds on the wrong things for the wrong reasons.

Cultures that don't work become barriers or brakes on your strategy or transformation efforts. In contrast, cultures that work become enablers and accelerators. If you're wondering why changes you're trying to make aren't working or great ideas aren't cutting through, your culture is probably getting in the way. If you're wondering why the strategy that makes sense in the boardroom or around the executive table isn't translating to the front line, your culture could be working against you. It doesn't matter

> Cultures that work enable and accelerate change efforts.

how great your strategy is; nothing will change if your culture isn't working for you.

Cultures have a vibe, a feeling that you can sense by interacting with anyone who works there. While the difference between good and great cultures is more nuanced, you'll know quickly whether or not a culture is working.

Asset or liability

Your culture can be your greatest asset or greatest liability. Culture may be intangible, but its impacts are not.

Didier Elzinga, founder and CEO of Culture Amp, believes that to succeed, you must put culture first. Culture Amp's mission is to grow Culture First companies. He says, 'Brand is a promise to a customer; culture is how you deliver that promise.'[7] Elzinga isn't saying purpose or profits don't matter, but rather that culture is the means to success. Culture First organisations recognise that investing in your capacity to respond to whatever comes makes sense in a world where you can't see what is around the corner.

Good cultures attract great people. Cultures that work grow and retain great people. Talent always has options. Culture helps you build a team that everyone wants to join. According to talent company Glassdoor's 2019 Mission and Culture Survey, almost 80% of workers consider a company's culture when looking for a job. And nearly 50% of employees would leave their current job for a lower-paying opportunity at an organisation with a better culture.[8]

A sense of belonging, connection, and feeling that your contribution is valued can become a flywheel for performance and retention. Your employer brand brings your culture to life for current and prospective team members. People want to stick around because cultures that work are worth belonging to.

Cultures that work are high performing. PwC's 2021 Global Culture Survey explored the link between culture and competitive advantage.[9] They found organisations with distinctive cultures enjoyed three key benefits: adaptability, collaboration and decision-making. PwC concluded that 'Organisations with a view of culture as a distinction and source of competitive advantage maintain a sense of community better, respond to customer needs better, innovate with a higher degree of success and deliver better business results'.

Cultures that work create financial value. The Institute for Corporate Productivity (i4cp) researched culture and high-performance organisations in 2018-2019. They found that, in terms of revenue growth, market share, profitability and customer satisfaction, organisations with healthy cultures were 3 times more collaborative, 2.5 times more innovative and 2.5 times more likely to view failure as an opportunity to learn and grow.[10] These organisations scored 3.5 times better when bringing the best out in their employees and 4 times better on empowering employees.

> Cultures that work enable better decision-making.

Cultures that work enable better decision-making. Strategies or policies can never anticipate everything. Culture fills in the gaps and shapes the decisions of leaders and team members. Cultures that work drive connection with the customer, whether in consumer (B2C) or business-to-business (B2B). They drive the right focus and behaviour.

> # Cultures that work learn and deliver at pace.

Cultures that work are adaptable, resilient, and have the capacity for readiness for what is around the corner. In times of crisis, cultures that work can respond in an agile way without relying on top-down direction. In my experience, cultures that work often look beyond their own needs and concerns to support those around them. Toxic cultures are more likely to be inward-focused or competitive, neither of which pays dividends in a crisis. There are countless examples from the early months of the global pandemic in 2020, where organisations with cultures that work came together and did what was required.

Cultures that work learn and deliver at pace. Creativity and innovation require a culture of embracing experimenting, learning from failure and rapid regrouping. Cultures that work against you often fear failure and lack psychological safety. Pace requires smooth running, continuous improvement, and commitment to outcomes. Cultures that work against you have friction in processes, poor communication and silo-bound teams that slow execution. You are more likely to see people working in flow, reduced friction, and cross-boundary collaboration in cultures that work.

Management consulting company Gallup's 2022 article on organisational culture calls out four key benefits. The article points out that culture attracts world-class talent, creates alignment, focuses engaged employees and affects performance.[11] Gallup's research shows that understanding company purpose and culture is directly linked to measures of business health. Their data indicates that doubling (from 40% to 80%) the number of employees who agree that the purpose of their organisation makes them feel their job is important, would see a 41% reduction in absenteeism, a

50% drop in safety incidents and a 33% improvement in quality measures. Gallup recommends leaders focus their cultural efforts on strengths, diversity and inclusion, safety, innovation, compliance and high performance for the maximum impact on their bottom line.

Cultures that work are valuable. Like goodwill, culture is an intangible asset. Unlike goodwill, it will never appear on a balance sheet. Without going into technical valuation principles involving multiples, replacement costs, discounted cash flows and such, goodwill is simply determined as the difference between the value of the tangible assets (property, plant, equipment, etc.) and the value of the company as a whole. So, for example, if a business is worth $2 billion and holds $1 billion in tangible assets, then goodwill would be valued at $1 billion.

In principle, goodwill grows as the company's value grows; however, technically, it is only measured and officially recognised on the balance sheet at the time of purchase. Unfortunately, there is no way to calculate the financial value of culture, but there has been some work done on the business case for culture. Professional services firm Grant Thornton's work with Oxford Economics, *Return on Culture*, is a good starting point if you wish to understand more.[12]

While there is important work to be done at an organisational level, the role of leaders shifting the culture in their teams shouldn't be underestimated. You don't need to wait for the broader organisation to start working on your culture before you can have an impact. Focus on what you can influence and control. If you shift the culture in your team, you can start a movement. Connect and collaborate with other leaders to gain momentum.

The aim of this book is to provide tangible actions to shift your culture. Investing in culture pays dividends. You can impact your culture by taking these actions every day and shifting your focus to daily culture. Move your culture from ugly to united, from uniform to unique, from the usual to useful. Shift your culture to work for you, not against you. Make your culture work.

> # Investing in culture pays dividends.

When your culture works for you, it becomes an asset that benefits all.

Shifting expectations

So, why now?

More than ever, leaders are expected to be worth following, to lead cultures worth belonging to and work worth doing, while investing in technology (and managing the distracting side effects) and dealing with shifting societal and regulatory demands. All while delighting customers, keeping teams safe, sustaining growth, and delivering results. It's a big ask.

As Lisa Kaye[13], leader of Learning and Organisational Development at Arup, says, 'leadership is relentlessly contextual'. The backdrop for leaders is increasing complexity and pace, ongoing ambiguity and uncertainty, and greater expectations from both inside and outside the organisation.

Peter Hinssen is the author who coined the phrase, the New Normal. He talks to organisations about the importance of preparing for a series of seismic shocks and thriving in the never-normal. The four seismic shocks Hinssen identifies are technological, biological (hello pandemic), ecological and geopolitical. These shocks lead to systemic shifts.

Consider the impact of digital on consumer behaviour and shifts in social media. Technology, automation, and AI (artificial intelligence) are rapidly encroaching on white- and blue-collar work. Rapid technological advances that see consumers trading in their iPhones every two to three years have shifted team members' expectations of the quality, currency and speed of their technology experience at work.

In addition to work dynamics, Hinssen forecasts shifts in business and operating models and the capacity and resources to deliver these. Add in expected volatility in economic and financial performance, and we need to increase our leaders' and organisational capacity to navigate the never-normal to be well-placed to pursue the opportunities in these systemic shifts. Peter Hinssen says culture is a key differentiator. He believes that to thrive in the New Next we need cultures with VACINE — an acronym that stands for Velocity, Agility, Creativity, Innovation, Network and Experimentation.[14]

As the world changes shape, so does the world of work. I recently read the suggestion that the shifts of the last decade in the workplace are like moving from high school to university. That resonates for many workplaces, but not all. It's been interesting to track the evolving dialogue and how organisations have grappled with the shifts to hybrid work. Some have coped better than others.

Of course, this shift was already on a continuum for knowledge workers, with one end in Silicon Valley with the unicorns and soonicorns, (some of whom were founded as fully remote organisations) and the other end in high visibility, FaceTime focused cultures.

People are looking for different. People are looking for more.

Largely ignored in the dialogue have been the operational or site-based organisations where team members are physically required to present to work, such as healthcare, retail, energy, manufacturing, construction and mining. Such organisations have been grappling with their own dynamics against a media backdrop of debates about how many days should be spent in the office. Many leaders and teams operating in these environments have felt invisible and ignored. This is at a time when society has become acutely aware of the importance of frontline workers in delivering key services, particularly in communities experiencing lockdowns during the pandemic.

Organisations have grappled with the transition from work as a place we go, to work as what we do. Interestingly, pre-pandemic, there was already a divide between how executives and team members viewed location. Insights from Grant Thornton's 2019 collaboration with Oxford Economics[15] highlighted that while 57% of executives thought a pleasing work environment was critical to employee loyalty and intention to stay, only 36% of team members thought so. In the US, the average cost of workplace renovation per employee was US$39,500. Since these figures in 2019, organisations have reviewed their footprint, with many downsizing their office holdings. Now, given the new ways of working, office refurbishments are focused on fit-for-purpose fitouts.

Flexibility in location and hours have not been the only workplace shifts. The deal has changed. Over the last decade, there has been a trend towards the casualisation of the workforce and an increase in the gig economy. More people are looking for autonomy and choice.

While the millennial generation has a reputation for job hopping, tenures in roles and at organisations are shortening across all generations.

The year 2021 was dubbed The Great Resignation or The Great Reshuffle and saw an expected spike in people hunting for new positions following two years of uncertainty. It also saw talent opting out of the professional job market altogether. Collectively, we have experienced a great re-evaluation. People are looking for different. People are looking for more. Redefining the nature of work, now dubbed the anti-work movement (AWM), people are turning their backs on long hours spent climbing the corporate ladder with poor job quality and are seeking greater purpose and impact in their work. Combined with a reduction in skilled immigrants (certainly in Australia and New Zealand), the talent crunch has impacted organisations across most sectors.

Culture as brand

While employer branding has always had strong links to culture, the evolution of marketing and brands over the last 15 years has implications for leaders and organisations shifting culture. The rise of cultures as brands and the emergence of team members as consumers, have introduced new ways of thinking about how we connect team members with our organisation.

Like culture, brands are intangible assets. The rise in consumer data and analytics has stayed ahead of the same work in organisational culture. The shift in expectations about what and when data is available has flowed into

> Like culture, brands are intangible assets.

organisational culture. Leaders and team members seek real-time data on team member sentiment. Network analytics, courtesy of natural language processing and boosted by the more recent rapid uptake of online meetings, is delivering new and timely insights into ways of working and team dynamics. The Microsoft Workplace Index has provided rich insights into how we gather and shifts in connections intra- and inter-teams.[16]

Consumers today are increasingly savvy and generally more brand aware. Trust has been eroded in institutions, and expectations of brands have expanded beyond the simple promise of a product. Consumers expect brands to take a position on social issues, and we've seen the rise of advocacy and activist brands. These expectations influence what current and prospective team members expect from their employers.

Global management consulting firm McKinsey's report *Purpose: Shifting from Why to How*[17] says, 'Employees are agitating for decisions and behaviours that they can be proud to stand behind and gravitating toward companies that have a clear, unequivocal and positive impact on the world.' And there is no single, homogenous view of what is right and expected. The explosion of niche causes and fragmentation of societal beliefs and values has exacerbated the expectation of taking a position and having a voice.

Social media has contributed to the diversity of opinions and the amplification of societal expectations. Shifts in what is socially acceptable have caught many an established organisation off guard. Cancel culture is playing out inside organisations, not just in Hollywood and celebrities in other fields. What once were accepted practices, such as non-disclosure agreements in the case of sexual harassment claims, are now required to be transparent. Organisations that do not keep up with or stay ahead of these shifts in expectations face active campaigning from customers and team members alike.

One of the greatest changes is the impact of hyper-personalisation in the workplace experience. There was only one television in my home when I was growing up. Viewing was restricted to whatever my parents watched during the week, and on Friday evenings, we watched a family movie together. We took turns choosing which to watch from the four available channels. As a teenager, the advent of VHS meant the family might rent a couple of movies each week. There were many negotiations with my little brother or sister in the aisles of the video rental shop Blockbuster about which movie was coming home with us.

When I began work, I expected a one-size-fits-all experience with allowances for some negotiation. It could be argued that the generation before me had expected one-size-fits-the-boss. Contrast that with someone who has only ever experienced music and media on streaming platforms with absolute choice over what they watch and when — usually on their personal device.

Consumers today receive personalised emails and ads from brands shaped by their shopping and browsing history. Mention camping in a conversation at home, and within half an hour, your Facebook and Google ads are full of tents and sleeping bags. People are conditioned to hyper-personalisation. None more so than the digital native millennials and the generations who follow them into the workplace.

A one-size-fits-all employee experience will not make a positive impression. Policies and practices that leave no room for discretion or differentiation will frustrate team members and negatively impact your culture. In a competitive talent market, your value proposition for team members must allow for a personalised experience throughout the employment life cycle.

Some say we are in an experience economy. Culture will become even more critical for attracting and retaining talent when organisations compete on their people experience.

We are in an experience economy.

Against this backdrop of shifts in the world and the world of work, culture can be an asset in delivering on these expectations and beyond.

Culture is having a moment

Culture is certainly having a moment. In recent years, Australia has seen several high-profile Royal Commissions and reviews into institutions ranging from aged care to banking and the public sector to the defence force, all of which have implicated culture in one way or another.

Peak bodies such as the Australian Institute of Company Directors (AICD) and the Australian Stock Exchange (ASX) have issued good practice guides on governing and managing culture. From tone from the top[18] to letting the sunshine in,[19] each review has found its own way to define culture and detail how to manage it. At last, culture is on the agenda.

With culture having a moment and increased demands on boards to address cultural concerns, accounting and governance firms are expanding into culture work, bringing their particular brand of heavy quantitative approach.

Culture audits and dashboards are selling well into corporate

Australia. Unfortunately, this sets up organisations for a fall. It offers a false sense of control. Boards will be able to happily trundle along ticking the culture box with an annual report that shows mostly green and a couple of quick wins they can address to show they are investing in culture.

Sadly, culture doesn't fit neatly into dashboards. Culture work requires both art and science. Of course, after decades of academics and experts positioning culture as either complex, stuffy, academic theory or fluffy, team building and employee satisfaction, a bit of rigour is appealing. The business case for culture has now evolved into a *return* on culture.[20]

Into this mix, add talent shortages, seismic shifts in ways of working, declines in workforce well-being, a yearning for connection and leaders seeking answers. Everybody wants to work on their culture. To top it off, now we have executives and boards who learned to lead by walking around, unable to see their teams working. No wonder the demand for culture work has exploded.

Culture will take you further than strategy can imagine

For the last three decades, culture has been positioned as an enabler of strategy. Its importance was recognised, but strategy remained the ultimate goal. I believe this is limiting.

Strategy is a gamble. We cannot predict the future. We cannot see around corners. Organisations desire a culture that enables their strategy, but this limits their potential and readiness for what is coming. Culture can provide readiness for the unknown better than any strategy. With increased volatility and uncertainty, horizons for strategies are shrinking. What used to be a five-year strategy is now a three-year strategy. What used to be a three-year strategy is now a 12-month one.

> ## While strategies can be copied, culture cannot.

My friend, Alex Hagan, writes and speaks on complexity, confusion and change in the New Normal.[21] He argues that strategies need to be adjusted and keep evolving, and he's right. Strategy and culture are both important and need to be monitored, adjusted and continually evolving. But while strategies can be copied, culture cannot. Culture provides the X factor. With the right people and a culture that works, organisations can go further than any strategy imagined today.

Remember, culture can be your greatest asset or your greatest liability. Culture can take you further. It's time to get your culture working for you.

What Is Culture Anyway?

Simplifying culture

With over a billion internet search results for definitions of culture, ranging from esoteric to #culcha, a single definition of culture is as slippery as culture itself.

Before we debate what culture is, and isn't, let's first debunk a few myths.

Culture is static

Culture is not static. It is dynamic, constantly swirling and shifting. Unlike Kurt Lewin's ice block theory of change which suggests we unfreeze, change and refreeze things,[1] culture is not frozen or fixed. One person can influence your culture. Some shifts are little ripples; some are quivers that evaporate as quickly as they arrive. Some ripples create lasting changes long after the person has left, or the story of what happened is forgotten.

The iceberg model is often misattributed to Edgar Schein, an MIT professor known for his ground-breaking work on organisational culture. In fact, it was developed by the American anthropologist Edward T Hall in the mid-1970s. The model positions culture with some visible above the waterline but most invisible below.[2] Like an iceberg, cultures do develop organically over time, but they are more fluid than ice.

> ## Cultures are active, not stagnant.

Cultures are active, not stagnant. Each individual contributes to the culture they find themselves in, and the relationship between members is symbiotic. That is why everyone is responsible for culture, not just the leader. Each person shapes and influences their culture – some more than others – whether by dint of power or personality. The culture shifts as each person joins or leaves, and sometimes stories and habits outlast the people who initiated them.

In 2022, I worked with a client to shift the levels of bureaucracy and safekeeping that had moved beyond a cultural strength to become a cultural shadow impacting decision-making and performance. I was told by many of those interviewed that the problem was the legal team slowing decisions down. Every key decision required a paper to the leadership team, and every paper had to pass through the legal team first.

During conversations with people across the organisation, I uncovered why people believed things had to be this way.

Five years earlier, the company had received a negative audit report. The recommendations included a legal review of key decisions to assess compliance risk. Over time, this evolved into reviewing all leadership team papers, which, of course, required a larger legal team.

The larger legal team sent papers back to the writers asking for more detail on risks resulting in heavier, more detailed papers. This increased the burden of reading on the leadership team, leaving less time for discussion and collaborative decision-making. New leaders joined the leadership team. New lawyers joined the legal team. Then, a template was developed to make it easier to review all the papers. This streamlined template stripped away the richness of the written papers, making the reading a chore.

Frustration built. Decisions were slower and required rework and follow-up. Leaders and lawyers changed, and the reason for the decision-making process was lost, yet the habit continued. What had started as a good idea became hardwired. Frustration and resentment grew. Decision-making was slower and more arduous.

Time moved on. Changes were made. The incoming CEO and new leadership team wanted to refresh the culture and build readiness for their new independence. Unearthing the story behind the layers of reasoning allowed a reset by the leadership team and was embraced by the legal team. Like scraping off layers of old paint to find beautiful wooden floorboards, getting to why and sharing the story enabled the required shift.

Culture is homogenous

Culture has been written about and discussed as a monoculture for too long. Whether national or organisational culture, our efforts to make it easier to understand have led to oversimplification. Sometimes how we describe culture almost makes it a parody.

Centuries of humour and war have been driven by our clumsy simplification of culture. Monoculture is a myth.

> If everyone behaves exactly the same way, it's a cult, not a culture.

Your culture is not homogenous — it's not yoghurt! If everyone behaves exactly the same way, it's a cult, not a culture. Cultures that work have healthy subcultures that are celebrated, not just accepted. Differences between the people, the work and the location contribute to healthy diversity in your culture. Within the macroculture, there will be microcultures.

Within any group, there are tribes and sub-cultures. Monocultures suffocate individual differences, whereas the rich diversity of cultures allows room for people to breathe and find their own way to belong. In an era of hyper-personalisation, this is increasingly important.

While a baby boomer might have sought the solidarity of a single set of values, organisations recognise that today people have a greater diversity of personal values and beliefs. A single set of organisational values, with a locked-down definition of associated behaviours, doesn't leave room for the individual. We increasingly work with principles, tenets, commitments, attributes, anchors and purpose to articulate culture. These terms create space for team members to belong.

Cultures that work reflect the work of the team. Logically, different ways of working will suit different functions within an organisation. While the logistics and distribution teams will focus on safety, efficiency, continuous improvement, and responsiveness, it's entirely appropriate that the marketing team focuses on creativity, engagement and partnering. The finance and legal teams will undoubtedly pay attention to what matters most to them. While the broader organisational culture will concentrate on what is shared across all teams, individual teams will also have their own interpretations.

Subcultures don't mean working in silos is acceptable. Working across boundaries is critical to the success of your organisation. Cross-functional teams have greater power and potential than homogenous, siloed teams.

What makes your culture distinctive is the unique mix of subcultures that, when combined, create something truly individual. Like a mosaic image made up of thousands of photos, it's impossible to replicate.

Culture operates in a vacuum

Your culture does not operate in a vacuum. Your organisation is not surrounded by a moat. External factors influence your current and future environments. The walls of your organisation are porous. The outside will come in, and your culture will flow out through interactions with customers and the community.

> Your culture does not operate in a vacuum.

When discussing culture, it is easy for leaders to focus purely on internal factors such as leaders, systems, constraints and tensions between teams. I've been in intense conversations with leadership teams committed to shifting their culture where external factors have been completely forgotten. More commonly, when designing and choosing the culture they desire, leadership teams tend to ignore outside influences such as regulations, unions and regional cultures.

Let's use your local Australian Coles supermarket as a case in point. When you visit Coles, you probably aren't thinking about the company's culture. If you're like me, you're concentrating on getting in and out as quickly as possible, grabbing the few items you came for. Your regular supermarket probably feels familiar.

Despite years of travel, I now live in the suburb next to my original family home. I shop at the same Coles as I did growing up. Sure, I've seen plenty of changes in the layout, products and purchasing process over the decades, but it still has the same general feel.

Occasionally I'll pop into another Coles to pick up something on the way home, but other than navigating a different layout, it still feels familiar. However, visiting Coles in Broome, Mt Isa, or Sydney CBD has a distinctly different feel. The physical layout isn't the only thing; it's the greetings and interactions with team members. The presence of the community in which the supermarket operates is visible in subtle and not-so-subtle ways. The vibe of the place is influenced by its surroundings.

Dynamic, healthy cultures are not threatened by regional flavours or regulatory impact. Cultures that work are strong enough to retain their core no matter the external influences. Broken cultures stifle, reject or shame difference because it is mistaken for a threat. Healthy cultures celebrate unique differences across regions. These, in turn, enrich the organisational culture. Cultures that work learn and grow over time as they respond to external shifts.

Culture is not experienced evenly

Culture is a shared experience, but it is not experienced evenly. Executives and leaders don't experience the organisation's culture in the same way as the workforce. The culture you experience is shaped by the power and status associated with the chair you sit in. As a leader, you typically have more autonomy and authority, which means you encounter the processes and controls of your organisation differently. You probably have access to information and context that your teams don't.

> Culture is a shared experience, but it is not experienced evenly.

Research shows that the higher you go in the hierarchy of an organisation, the more likely you feel closer to the purpose and strategy of the organisation. Unsurprisingly, 84% of executives agree they can pursue their professional goals and personal passions without too much difficulty, yet only 69% of team members say the same.[3] Intuitively this makes sense. However, it can highlight the experience gap when you consider what this means for how you, as a leader, experience culture. Gartner's research into the gaps between executive and employee sentiment found that while 75% of executives felt they listened to their people, only 47% of team members felt listened to.[4]

Depending on your role, your experience of the culture may be so cleansed that you experience the Disney version, protected from the underbelly. As an executive across multiple brands and multiple locations, it is easy to stay in the vetted, cleansed world presented to you. I have often had to actively search for team members on the front line to talk to me about what is really happening. So, the culture you experience is not the same as those experienced by your team. It might be time to consider that perhaps you don't know your culture as well as you think you do.

Different teams don't experience your culture evenly. We know leaders have an outsized impact on culture. If you look around your peers, each leader brings their own style, personality and preferences to their way of leading. Add functional and accountability differences, and how you lead will be at least 20% different from those around you. Even if there is only a 10% difference, the resulting culture in their team will be at least 10% different from yours.

It's not something we spend a lot of time thinking about.

The myth of the monoculture has contributed to this. Solid and healthy cultures can withstand differences in leadership styles as long as there is alignment on what matters most.

> ## How we comprehend the world is influenced by our unique perspectives.

Even within your team, people don't experience your culture evenly. Like everything, how we comprehend the world is influenced by our unique perspectives, shaped by our upbringing, life experience, education and knowledge, and our attitude on the day. Imagine you and I are standing side-by-side, looking at a waterfall. While viewing the same thing, we experience the waterfall differently due to our mix of personal filters, preconceptions and perceptions. The same happens with culture. Three people in the same team, office or pod working on the same tasks will experience the culture differently because of their backgrounds, biases, filters and perceptions.

This reinforces the importance of making your culture real by linking it to everyday behaviours, giving examples, and letting teams experience and discuss what it means to them.

Culture is the reason (the blame game)

It has become a thing to blame culture for any organisational failures. As Margaret Heffernan writes in *Beyond Measure: The Big Impact of Small Changes*, when confronted with spectacular failure, everyone points in the same direction — the culture.[5]

For me, this is a case of 'yes, and'. When reviewing failures, it is not enough to blame culture and stop there. Whether it is sexual harassment in the military or mining, fraud in banking or cheating in cricket, we need to look beyond the culture to the systems that drove the behaviour. Look to the individuals, the habits and the rewards (intended or otherwise) that led to the issues. A powerful exploration of this is Samantha Crompvoets' book *Blood Lust, Trust and Blame*,[6] following her review of culture in Australia's Defence Force. Blaming culture rather than specific individuals or systems is not enough to achieve the required shifts.

I don't rant often. In fact, one of my mentors would say I don't rant often enough. However, one thing that might trigger a rant is the phrase 'a few bad apples'. A media article or regulator report will often blame and call for the removal of a handful of individuals who have caused problems. While acting swiftly and fairly on individual misconduct is important, the issue will reoccur unless the systems that enabled or encouraged the behaviour are dismantled or adjusted. New 'bad apples' will simply replace the old.

Blaming individuals instead of the culture doesn't achieve the required shifts. When it comes to conduct risk, I recommend that boards and the executive address the individuals *and* the culture. Tackling only one will not address the issue. We need to address the root cause and deal with the symptoms. Culture may be to blame, but to do something about it, we need more.

Culture can be copied and pasted

No culture is perfect, and there is no such thing as the ideal culture for your organisation. Besides, we know that a perfect culture isn't a culture; it's a cult.

No culture is perfect. It is, after all, inherently a human system. Striving for perfection implies there is an end state or destination culture. Since cultures are dynamic and constantly shifting, it is better to regard them as works in progress.

> ## You can't copy someone else's culture.

You can't copy someone else's culture, transplanting a culture from one organisation to another. Organisations have different cultures, their customers and origins are different and different motivations often drive their people. If you are going to adopt an element of another culture into your own, make sure it is a considered action. Like adopting a puppy for Christmas, think through the ramifications and adaptations to achieve the right fit.

While you can adopt and adapt ways of working, rituals, or symbols from other organisations you admire, your unique combination and application make your culture. Every organisation should find its own.

There is no one way to do culture.

If your culture is working for you, then protect, nurture and maintain your focus on it. Cultures that work will naturally evolve and develop. Don't be distracted by other organisations' cultures. While there are certainly wrong ways, there are many right ways to shape, shift and lead culture. Go with what works for your culture and for your organisation.

> Go with what works for your culture.

Culture is...

If you're looking for a universally accepted definition of culture, this book is not for you. Instead, let's explore together what culture is and is not.

Here are some simple and useful descriptors that help set the scene.

- Culture is what people repeatedly do.
- Culture is the way we do things around here.
- Our culture is what makes us, us.

I asked 50 leaders to define culture – here are some of their responses.

An organisation's culture is defined by its stories.
Chris Morsley[7]

Culture is what defines the soul of an organisation.
Keana Hunter[8]

A culture exists when a group of people share views – manifested in patterns of behaviour – about 'what's right (and also wrong) around here'.
Paul McAuley [9]

If an organisation is an engine and people are its fuel, culture greases everything.
Julia Steel[10]

Culture is the 'we' of a team and how each 'I' contributes.
David French[11]

How and why we do things, how we treat each other, what is important, what are our rituals?
Katherine Hoepper[12]

The way things happen around here.
Lana Johnston[13]

The unwritten rules that everyone just seems to know.
Tara Kleine[14]

Culture is about expected behaviour. Good or bad, expectations drive the way people think, feel and act. They ultimately determine reality. Culture impacts everyone and everything at every level.
Karlie Webster[15]

Culture is how performance is delivered within an organisation.
Alex Staley[16]

The values, beliefs and actions of a collective.
Tanya Hill[17]

Behaviours and beliefs guide how an organisation's management and employees work together and handle business transactions.
Andrew Matuszczak[18]

Culture is the values and characteristic set of behaviours that define how things get done in an organisation.
Andrew Steele[19]

How people think and behave translates into their actions. It's the underlining fabric of how things get done, connecting people to business strategy.
Aidan Read[20]

The way the organisation works.
Anita Hobson-Powell[21]

It's the heartbeat of the workplace; it influences how people perform in an organisation and what values and attitudes the team accepts and works by.
Nathan Reibel[22]

Anthropologists, sociologists, academics of many flavours and business leaders (like me) have been trying to land useful definitions of culture for more than a century. Defining organisational culture lands more than 45.5 million hits on Google.

According to Google Trends, the three most common search queries related to culture are: What is organisational culture? What is culture? Organisational culture definition. In 2014, culture was Merriam-Webster's word of the year.[23]

The word culture stems from the Latin verb *colore*, meaning to cultivate, nurture and protect. All jokes aside, it is related to the term *cult*, which is derived from the French *culte*, meaning worship, stemming from the Latin root *cultus*, meaning care, cultivation and worship.[24]

The Oxford Dictionary of Philosophy defines culture as a way of life, including the ideas, customs and social behaviour of a particular people or society.[25] It broadens beyond their attitudes, values and beliefs to include modes of perception and habits of thought and activity. Cultures are learned but are often too pervasive to be easily noticed from within. Put simply, cultures are caught, not taught, and they're hard to see when you're in them. Replace 'way of life' with 'way of working', and this translates well into organisational culture.

> Cultures are caught, not taught.

I worked with frontline leaders at the coalface (literally, in coal mines out in the pit), answering their question, 'What is culture anyway?' I'd answer, 'It's how things get done around here.' I'd say, 'It's the stories we tell and our unwritten rules.' Culture is why someone who is a hero over the road (the competitor's mine was on the other side of the highway) is seen as a villain here. While you can't see or touch it, you can feel it. I often invoked the classic Australian movie, *The Castle*.[26] It's the vibe of the place.

Defining culture

Culture is the foundation on which all other aspects of an organisation are built, shaping how people think, feel and behave. It is a powerful force that influences an organisation's performance, productivity and overall success.

> Defn.: Culture is the shared values, beliefs, norms, patterns and practices that define an organisation.

But what does that mean in everyday language?

Theory	Everyday Language
Shared values	What matters most
Beliefs	Unwritten rules Myth busting
Norms	What good looks like What is acceptable
Patterns	Habits (thinking and doing) Repeated activities or behaviours
Practices	What we do

Underlying beliefs, assumptions and accepted norms shape team member behaviour more than formal policies and procedures. Culture is formal and informal, tangible and intangible.

I've heard culture described as ecosystems and operating systems. These are helpful metaphors if we aren't practised in systems thinking. In ecosystems and operating systems, elements interact with and reinforce each other. A systems thinking approach recognises that the sum is greater than its parts; all the pieces of an organisation connect, interact and play a role in outcomes. Applying systems thinking will help you understand how the disparate elements come together to form the culture you experience today.

> Culture is formal and informal, tangible and intangible.

It can be useful to think of culture as a technology stack, where some layers are older, legacy elements, and some are more stable and stickier. Some layers in your culture stack are well-established, while others are new and need embedding. Some are emerging, while others are crumbling away. Some need nurturing and protecting, and others need to be refreshed and updated. There are layers that are essential and layers that need to be replaced. Like your technology ecosystem, culture is multi-faceted, interconnected and dynamic. And, like your tech stack, culture requires ongoing investment and maintenance.

Culture is cumulative; it is an accumulation of moments. Each person, gathering, ritual, action, symbol and story piles on top of the ones before, like thousands of snowflakes. I find this analogy helpful as each snowflake is unique and individual, but multiple layers of snowflakes make a blanket of snow. Perhaps a better analogy in Australia is a beach. Each grain of sand is individual, but many layers create a beach. Anthropologists regard human cultures as cumulative.[27] Generally, we learn from and build on the generations

> # Culture is cumulative; it is an accumulation of moments.

and civilisations before us. The same applies to organisations. Sometimes we learn from history, but sometimes we forget the lessons and are doomed to repeat them.[28]

Culture is also accretive. That is, it increases gradually, although that change can be positive or negative. Toxic cultures creep and can be insidiously deep-rooted before they become apparent to leaders and boards. Broken cultures are often in a destructive loop or a vicious circle, requiring an intervention and a reset. Good cultures are value accretive – they become a virtuous circle. The challenge for leaders is often to sustain the positive uplift over time.

Culture happens

Like politics, culture happens once you have more than two people together. If you're reading this book, you probably understand and accept that your organisation has a culture now, whether through default or design and whether or not you were part of its creation.

Much of my organisational culture work is with boards, CEOs and executive teams. I work one-on-one with executives and leadership teams. While I've created a diagnostic to assess the current state of an organisation's culture, our partnership focuses on co-designing their chosen culture and determining the shifts required to move the organisation towards it. This work does not involve moving an organisation from black to white, but rather from shades of grey to further shades of grey. It's about developing more of some things and less of others. It's about priorities and prevalence rather than perfection. Culture work is ongoing; it requires shifting systems and everyday actions.

> ## Culture work is ongoing.

Simplifying culture for action

Simplicity vs complexity

The challenge for leaders and aspiring leaders is this: culture is complex. The American jurist and legal scholar Oliver Wendell Holmes once remarked, 'I could not give a fig for simplicity on this side of complexity, but I would give my left arm for simplicity on the other side of complexity.'[29]

Complex and complicated ideas require a lot of cognitive focus to digest and understand. Simple ideas can be understood with a minimum of effort. The fastest way to action is the most direct. For leaders to be able to action culture every day, it needs to be simple enough for all leaders to understand. To action culture, we need to ground it in everyday activities that leaders already do — or could do.

Einstein famously said things should be as simple as possible and no simpler. In my efforts to make culture actionable for leaders, I have developed a simple way of thinking about a complex thing. Part Two of this book will step you through my GRASS model.

GRASS is grounded in what leaders can action every day and concentrates on what research tells us has the greatest impact on culture. As some of my mining mates say, these are the things that punch above their weight.

Culture is actionable

Cultures that work are built and reinforced in the everyday, where culture happens.

> # Cultures are best shifted in the everyday.

Cultures are best shifted in the everyday. One-off announcements, events and experiences are great to kickstart and accelerate momentum; however, unless your teams experience culture shifting, the half-life of any information or event will dwindle until they are forgotten. Culture lives in the day-to-day experience of your team.

No matter how amazing your onboarding swag or online learning programs, group-wide initiatives only work when the groundswell of leaders adopt the habits of the chosen culture.

How you work and lead can shift the culture of your team and those around it. Connect with your peers and colleagues and create a cascade of action.

By focusing on what matters most for your team, you can shift culture without calling on consultants in shiny suits to do an audit and create a dashboard.

Remember, culture may be complex, but it is understandable.

Culture may be intangible, but it is actionable.

Shifting Culture

Everyone contributes to culture

We all contribute to culture. It doesn't only exist while the CEO is watching. It lives every day in every team member's actions. The cumulative nature of culture means that the newest team member can impact the culture around them. Like skimming stones, each person sends out multiple small ripples. We've all experienced how much impact one person can have on a meeting or in a project team. One person can shift the vibe pretty quickly. Now multiply that across the organisation.

Working with teams at every level of the organisation is a critical part of shifting culture. When you shift the team's culture, you start to shift the organisation's culture. And the most powerful lever in the process is you.

Culture: whose job is it anyway?

Accountability. Some cultures say 'one throat to choke', while others talk about the directly responsible individual (DRI). Some

> # Everyone thinks it's someone else's job.

cultures develop a RASCI framework detailing who was responsible, who was accountable, who played a supporting role and who needed to be consulted or informed. When we need something done in organisations, we must determine who is accountable.

I'm frequently asked, 'Whose job is culture?'

One of the greatest threats to your culture is when everyone thinks it's someone else's job.

Culture is the CEO's job

We have all seen a CEO shift an organisation's culture — with support, of course. A single leader can impact how things are done through sheer personality and presence. As the CEO, you are ultimately accountable for your organisation's culture. While everyone contributes, your task is to lead and ensure that you and your leaders role-model the culture of choice. The CEO brings direction, drive, expectation and energy to the work of culture.

Culture is the board's job

Board governance and oversight roles place them squarely in the frame for ensuring that organisations monitor and manage their culture. Boards set the tone in the selection and support of the CEO and the standards they pay attention to. To misquote Tony Robbins, 'where your focus goes, their energy flows'.[1] Culture plays a role in the long-term success and sustainability of the organisation, and the board's role in guiding strategy, risk and opportunity requires an eye on culture. The board brings questioning, perspective and insight to the work of culture.

Culture is HR's job

The rebranding of human resources (HR) as people and culture hasn't helped confusion over accountability.

The HR team is well-placed to support leaders' efforts at different levels and their role as owners and designers of the many systems, frameworks and tools that impact culture. Not all systems affecting culture sit within the remit of HR, though. I prefer cross-functional teams working on culture, including subject matter expertise from HR.

Executive sponsorship is critical. When culture work is delegated too far, it risks becoming transactional rather than transformational. Not all HR teams are resourced with organisational development (OD) or organisational capability (OC) expertise. Within the HR world, these specialist domain skills are typically in-house in larger organisations. The shortage of experienced OD and OC practitioners across Australia and New Zealand is of concern. While the board may monitor culture, and the CEO and leadership team lead culture, the HR team bring their expertise and resources to culture work.

Culture is everybody's job

Culture is everybody's responsibility and opportunity. We all contribute to culture. We all know that person who impacts those around them, for better or worse. The key message I deliver when embarking on a Cultureshift program

We all contribute to culture.

with clients is that we all contribute to culture and that culture is the responsibility of us all.

Culture is your day job

While it is everybody's responsibility, it is the leader's job.

I believe that if you lead an organisation or a team, culture is your day job and an every day job.

You can't touch this

So now we know what culture is (and isn't). We know culture is important yet complex, and we know that it can be shifted. But how do you move something you can't touch?

One of the best examples of shifting something you can't touch is the Winter Olympic sport of curling. Here's a quick lesson.

Curling stone

Curling is a team sport played on ice, named for the rotational spin of the curling stone that causes it to take a curved path. Like culture, the stone never moves in a straight line. Curling requires a high degree of balance, precision and athleticism. Teams of four must move the stone (it weighs about 20kg) from one end of the alley to the other. After the initial push to start, the stone cannot be touched and is moved along by the initial momentum and the energy applied to the ice. Curlers sweep the ice ahead of the stone to help it travel further and straighter.

Sweeping reduces friction and helps the curlers control the amount of curl, straightening the stone's trajectory. Sweeping quickly heats and melts the ice leaving a film of water. The idea is to gently warm the surface of the ice where the stone will glide across. Good sweeping can allow a stone to travel two or three metres further.

Watching a curling team shift the stone along an alley five metres wide and 45 metres long at speed is fascinating. As best as I can tell, scoring appears to be a cross between darts and lawn bowls, with the stones closest to the button in the centre of the target scoring the most points. As an aside, one of the reasons I love curling is that, within the match, each team is allocated thinking time. What other sport does that?

Back to culture. Kicking off provides the initial momentum, and success is determined by the focus and energy of those doing the work. Although you can never actually touch culture, you can see the results of your efforts.

One of my clients, a state government-owned agency, talks about the impact of our Cultureshift work in terms of visible everyday shifts. From a quiet, siloed workplace, people now greet each other and mingle freely across teams. The language used by the teams has changed. They have adopted concepts like 'taking the oar' – used by the team to take ownership of a task, e.g., I've got the oar on this one. Managers now refer to themselves as leaders. Problem-venting sessions have morphed into problem-solving sessions. The energy, the vibe, is positive and upbeat.

Everything everywhere, all at once

I admit I haven't yet watched the movie of this name, but I love the title.[2] It sums up conversations I have had with leaders over the years. None of us has the time, resources or capacity to shift everything, everywhere, all at once. We need to consider our constraints and make choices. Thankfully, constraints drive creativity. Successful shifts in culture identify what to keep, what to refresh and what to leave behind.

When choosing what to focus on, I ask leaders to consider these five questions.

- What needs to be **retained**? What is working now? What are the positives or strengths you want to keep? What will still serve you in the future?

- What needs to be **refreshed**? What is good but needs reinvigorating? Perhaps a strength needs modernising? Or perhaps recommunicated?

- What needs to be **replaced**? What would be better left behind? What would you be better off without? What is outdated or no longer working for you?

- What is **required**? What parts of your culture are necessary for success today or in the future? What will you need that you don't have now? What will make this culture work for you?

- What could we **reach** for? For today or the future, what should we aspire to? What could make this a great place to work? What is on the edge of possible?

You can achieve a visible and felt shift by focusing on what matters now and what matters most. There's no need to do everything, everywhere, all at once.

Going meta for a minute

Wait, what if we need to change our culture, but to change our culture we need our culture to change.... It's easy to spin out here, but I want to dance lightly over this whirlpool so we don't get dragged down into its spiralling depths.

This is a real and valid concern for leaders. McKinsey's research shows that 70% of transformation projects fail, and some attribute up to 70% of the failure rate to culture.[3]

How we change culture is as important as what we are changing. As a dynamic system, working on one part will have flow-on effects. These may be planned or unplanned. While we can't control them, we must remain aware of the consequences and address any issues that may arise. We need to be considered and deliberate about how we change culture, not just what needs to change.

One paradox of culture is that it acts as both an anchor and a flywheel for change. Culture contributes to stability and creates inertia and resistance to change — both good and bad. Culture can act as a keel for your organisation through rough seas. Cultures that work buffer headwinds and smooth waves, but, like any overplayed strength, they can also be a source of weakness. Without deliberate effort, the natural weight of your culture can slow and even stop change in its tracks.

> **Harness the culture itself to help you shift.**

It's vital to harness the culture itself to help you shift. If your culture is naturally social and values fun, events can be a great way to start and sustain your shift. If your culture values evidence and expertise, include credible and experienced team members in your culture working group and ensure you have facts and figures in the stories you share. If your culture values community and partnerships, invite external stakeholders to help shape it. It's worth taking the time to consider how your current culture can be harnessed to enable and accelerate your shift. Do this well, and your culture can become a flywheel for change.

Everyday shifts

I'm passionate about democratising culture so leaders and organisations feel confident and competent to shift their culture. Acknowledging the need for expertise, guidance and support from experts such as myself, I focus on leaders feeling willing and able to take the lead. Success for me is walking alongside leaders as they shape, shift and sustain their culture to one that works.

While many shifts can (and need to be) made at an organisational or system level, there are everyday shifts that only you, as a leader, can make happen. Let's focus on actions leaders can take without relying on broader system changes which take time and investment.

As Emma Gibbens, change strategist and co-founder of Acknowledge This, says,

> 'Culture is what we participate in; how we
> show up every day. We change culture by
> being different and participating differently
> and that creates the ripples of change.'[4]

Follow the leader

The role of leaders in shaping and sustaining culture is critical. That means all leaders, not just the CEO. A single leader can change the way things are done around here. Think of a time when a team leader created an island of high performance in their team, despite what was happening in teams around them. Or perhaps you've seen how quickly a poor leader can undermine success and weaken a previously high-performing team.

I've worked for leaders who are magnets for talent and work with impact. They create an environment where everyone does great work, has a strong sense of purpose and is valued for their contribution.

I've also worked for leaders who were manic narcissists and ruthless sociopaths. They created environments where people felt unsafe, and politics, ego and aggression were rewarded. Most leaders, however, sit somewhere between these two book ends.

Leading culture is an everyday focus. It is an everyday activity that happens in every team across the organisation. Culture is the day job for leaders.

> # Leading culture is an everyday focus.

Google's Project Oxygen set out to test if managers still mattered.[5] The research confirmed the impact of leaders in teams and refreshed and expanded the original eight key behaviours to ten. As you might expect, these include coaching, decision-making, communicating and being productive and results-oriented. The Oxygen behaviours also include empowering the team, supporting career development and discussing performance, collaborating across the organisation and having a clear vision and strategy for the team.

Let's take these ten behaviours as a standard for the expected activity of a leader outside of the technical aspects of their role. They're what a leader does. Leading culture, then, is how you do what you do. Leading culture means deliberately doing what you do in a way that contributes to culture.

Shift culture every day

When it comes to our own development, we know that deliberate daily habits work better than radical changes.

There are many great thinkers and books out there, ranging from *Atomic Habits* by James Clear and BJ Fogg writing about *Tiny Habits,* to Jeff Olsen's *The Slight Edge* and Darren Hardy's *The Compound Effect.* Their message is clear; small shifts done consistently over time lead to greater and more sustainable change.[6] The same works for culture. And to quote one of my favourite songs, by Paul Kelly, 'From little things, big things grow'.[7]

Culture is best shifted where it is at. While there are moments of truth and events of cultural significance in each organisation, culture lives in the everyday. And it is in the everyday that the most sustainable changes occur. Aspirations and promises live in launch events, but the *delivery* occurs on the job.

> Culture is best shifted where it is at.

As a student of human behaviour, I'm fascinated by culture at work and at play. Reflect on your experiences of retreats, workshops, training courses, conferences and town hall events. How does the culture in the room or online at these events differ from the everyday? Sure, everyone is (usually) on their best behaviour but look beyond that. An intensity occurs when you bring people together, particularly if they are focused on one thing, such as a strategy, an opportunity, or a celebration. It's like when you dress up for a special occasion; you're still you, but you look a bit different than usual.

The energy of these events is valuable for shifting culture – it connects and aligns people to the collective effort and kicks off a sense of momentum. However, the energy can quickly fade once it hits day-to-day reality. How often have you attended training courses where you made commitments to do things differently and then forgot them once you returned to your day job? Maybe, like New Year resolutions, they lasted less than 20 days — research shows that only 11% of people keep their resolutions past the first month.[8] Shifts in culture require the energy and impetus to change, as well as everyday actions to sustain change.

So, for culture shifts to be sticky, they need to happen as you work. While I hope this book gives you new ideas for actions and experiments to try, for the most part, you will already be doing these actions as part of your day job. You already give feedback and direction, meet with your team, delegate tasks and develop your people. You already gather your people, practise rituals, take action, connect with symbols and share stories.

I challenge you to leverage these everyday moments for greater impact by doing them *on* purpose and *with* purpose. I hope you change it up, add a few new things to your toolkit and inspire your peers and team to do the same. By shifting how you think about your team, your culture and how you do your job every day, you're already on your way.

The good news is that your future culture is already here; it's just not evenly distributed yet.[9] Currently, there will be individuals and teams working the way you want your whole organisation to work. They are focused on doing the right things the right way. The first step is to identify, nurture and reward them. The second step is to connect them; it can sometimes be lonely for these individuals and teams. Knowing there are others on a similar path can re-energise

Shifting culture every day works.

these stars. Third, share their stories to promote these ways of working and encourage other teams to adopt them. Combine these steps with leadership messaging about the direction and shifts in your chosen culture, and you are on your way to gaining real momentum.

Everyday culture matters. Shifting culture every day works.

Remember, culture is your day job.

Cultureshift

Regardless of your starting point, a formula for shifting culture allows you to target your efforts on the elements of your culture that have the greatest impact. Even better, the Cultureshift formula works for organisation-wide initiative-led change and everyday leader-led change on the ground.

The Cultureshift formula

The formula is:

```
Moments that matter

x

Multipliers

=

Chosen culture
```

The Cultureshift formula

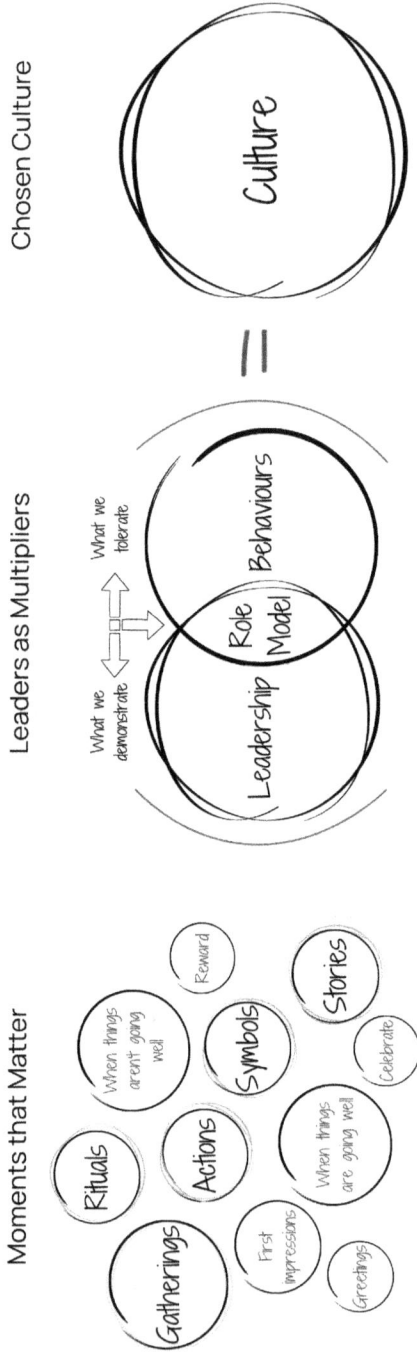

Chosen Culture

Culture

=

Leaders as Multipliers

What we demonstrate

What we tolerate

Leadership

Role Model

Behaviours

Moments that Matter

Rituals

Gatherings

Actions

First impressions

Greetings

When things aren't going well

Symbols

When things are going well

Reward

Stories

Celebrate

Moments that matter

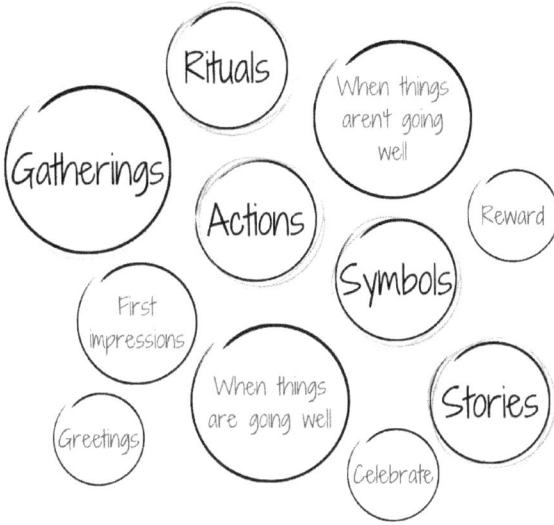

Culture is experienced as a series of moments that matter. Some moments matter more than others in how your team members see, feel and experience your culture. Some are small and encountered frequently by most team members, while only a few experience big moments.

Moments that matter include gatherings, first impressions and when things are and are not going well. These are all moments of truth where your undeniable culture becomes apparent. These moments punch above their weight to deliver an outsized impact. They have a significant effect on how people perceive your organisation and leadership.

> Some moments matter more than most.

When it comes to shifting culture, some moments matter more than most.

Multipliers

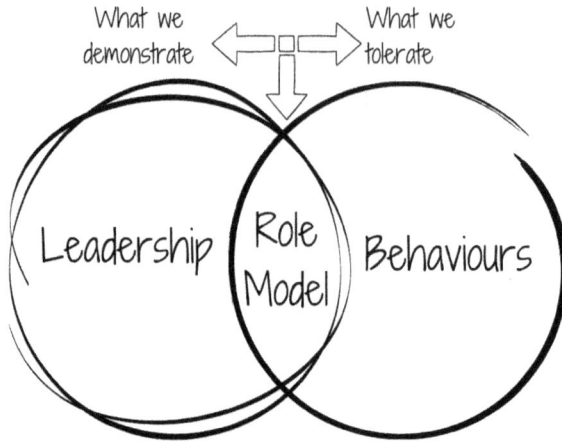

As a leader, you play an essential role in culture. You set the tone for the organisation. The behaviours you demonstrate and the behaviours you tolerate have a more significant impact than any shift in policy. The larger your team, the greater the impact. The most powerful part is played by you.

> ## What you model, ripples.

What you model, ripples. The ripple effect can't be contained or controlled. Most humans have a highly developed BS detector, or cognitive dissonance, which quickly identifies the gap between what is said and what is done.

Leadership acts as a multiplier in moments that matter. Positive multipliers amplify positive experiences, but negative multipliers can quickly negate them. Whether created by leaders or tolerated by them, a negative experience multiplied by negative behaviours deteriorates culture exponentially.

Simply put, your culture is shaped by the behaviours you reward and those you punish.

Your chosen culture

The design of your chosen culture is best shaped by what you desire and what you require. That is, what kind of culture you *want* and what kind of culture you *need*.

That is not to say you can erase your existing culture and aim for something completely unrecognisable. Your chosen culture should be recognisable from where you stand today. It's a new and improved version of you, but it's still you.

The final part of choosing your culture is identifying the shifts required to achieve it. These become the work to do.

The formula is:

Chosen culture

=

Required culture

+

Desired culture

+

Shifts from Current culture

Designing the culture you choose should be a team effort. It's best when co-created with representatives across different teams. It's important to articulate your aspirational culture in terms of what matters most, using language that resonates with your team. Involving leaders and influencers from across the organisation in shaping and shifting your culture leads to greater sustainability and stickability.

> ## Culture is always a work in progress.

Like all aspirations, our chosen culture may change as we get closer to it. That's ok, this work is never done. Culture is always a work in progress.

Focus your effort

The Cultureshift formula allows you to target your efforts for the greatest impact.

By focusing on shifting moments that matter and multipliers, your chosen culture becomes visible faster to team members. Delivering quick wins maintains momentum while clearing the way for deeper culture work. You can then properly invest in longer-term shifts requiring time and money, such as changes to organisational technology, systemic or infrastructure, to sustain the chosen culture.

Remember, your leadership multiplies moments that matter to achieve your chosen culture.

Part 2

GRASS

The Story Behind GRASS

I am passionate about simplifying culture for leaders so they feel confident and competent to shift their culture without relying on experts to do it for (or to) them.

I developed the Cultureshift formula you've just read about in Chapter Four based on my decades of experience working with leaders and organisations to shift culture. In culling a long list of moments that mattered, I landed on what has become Groundwork and GRASS.

I like grass. What kid doesn't love rolling down a grassy slope? Whether on a road trip through Australia or New Zealand or travelling by train through Europe, I always gaze out the window as the fields drift by. There are so many shades of green. I always look for parks in cities, too; they're great for reconnecting with nature and people-watching while sitting on the grass. As I'm married to a golfer, I've spent many days (he might say not enough) in a golf buggy enjoying the sunshine and the rolling greens of various courses. Saturday morning sports. Backyards in summer. Grass makes me think of happy times.

Grass also calls to mind a conversation with a great leader I worked with who, reflecting on his time leading operational teams, likened it to mowing the lawn. He said he could look over his shoulder and see what was cut and what was still to mow. He felt a sense of achievement at the end of each day and clarity about what was next. Our conversation has stayed with me.

Grass works as a useful metaphor for culture too.

Grass needs care and maintenance; it's not a one-and-done intervention. It can be wild or a well-trimmed lawn. Both are beautiful when they are healthy. Weeds can grow even in the best quality grass. There are plenty of varieties of grass. It can grow from seed or be imported as turf, or you can work with what you have. The grass looks greener on the other side, but it's greenest where you water it. A complex root system connects individual blades. You can develop a level of grass expertise, but there's nothing like the experience of looking after your own. There are grass experts and plenty of resources about grass, yet what matters most is how we treat our grass every day. Ok, so I could go on, but I won't. You get the picture.

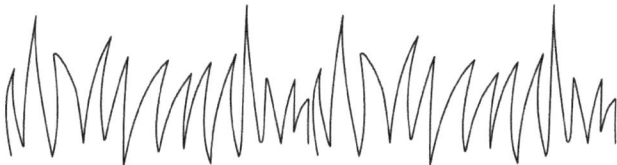

Shifting gears

It's time to shift gears as we move from understanding culture to actioning culture.

Part Two unpacks the GRASS model covering five areas, Gatherings, Rituals, Actions, Symbols and Stories, where you can take daily action to shift your culture.

Shifting gears.

First, though, I'll dig into the groundwork you'll need to do before you can focus on GRASS.

5

GRASS

I work with leaders and organisations. While this book is for leaders, I also reference organisation-wide steps to support and accelerate your culture shift. These typically require more time and investment, but they are not a barrier to starting to focus on your GRASS.

A leader's role

Remember what you read earlier; as a leader, you play an essential role in culture. The behaviours you demonstrate and the behaviours you tolerate have a more significant impact than any shift in policy. The larger or more visible your team, the greater your influence.

Your role in shifting culture includes making sense of the culture now, linking the threads to the past and leading shifts toward your chosen culture.

You are best placed to help your people make sense of the gap between the organisation's description of its culture and their day-to-day experience. Perhaps there are legacy or geographical reasons why the culture is different. Perhaps it is an acceptable gap, or maybe it isn't.

No matter how well-designed or supported the moments that matter, the way you action these moments influences the success of frameworks, systems and tools. The onboarding system and resources developed to support a team member's first 90 days might be woeful or wonderful, but you, as the leader, have the greatest effect on the integration and future success of your new starter. You are where it all comes together.

GRASS may mean you have to shift gears as a leader. You may need to rethink habits and unlearn practices built over your career.

Why are you bringing your people together? Are you reflecting on the unintended consequences of your behaviours? How often are you sharing stories?

As you become more aware of your practices, behaviours and the rituals and symbols around you, you'll need to move into an observer role to get a different perspective. Only then can you jump back in to act and shift toward your chosen culture.

Groundwork

There are three moments that always matter. I refer to these as doing the groundwork because they are universal and count in all relationships. We recognise and focus on these intuitively, so here's a quick mention before we move on to GRASS.

The three grounding moments are first impressions, when things are going well and when things aren't going well. As a new leader, these are a great place to start and get right. If you're an experienced leader, reflect on how you stack up in these three important foundations.

First impressions matter.

First impressions matter. Onboarding *really* matters; how new team members are welcomed and introduced to your organisation sets the tone for their entire tenure. A positive onboarding experience helps new team members feel valued and engaged, while a negative experience creates a sense of disconnection and disengagement.

Make sure that new team members have a clear understanding of your culture and what matters most. It is equally essential to provide new team members with the resources and support they need to be successful. Too many onboarding experiences focus on process and compliance rather than delivering an experience that sets people up for success. Turnover in the first year can often be traced back to poor onboarding.

Leaders are often assessed on how they lead when things are, and are not, going well. Positive feedback and recognition help team members feel valued and appreciated when things are going well, which can generate increased engagement and motivation. A lack of feedback or recognition can lead to disengagement and demotivation. Regular performance conversations and opportunities for feedback help team members understand how their work fits into the organisation's overall objectives and purpose. Recent data explored by employee experience platform Culture Amp showed that quarterly performance conversations are optimal alongside a culture of ongoing feedback.[1]

Dr Joel Davies, a senior people scientist at Culture Amp, said the data reveals that team members who have quarterly performance discussions are more likely to believe their manager is interested in their career aspirations and more likely to think that their job performance is evaluated fairly. He says quarterly performance discussions are also associated with more positive perceptions of reward and recognition at one's organisation.

Wins and wobbles

After first impressions, the two remaining grounding moments are when things are going well and when things aren't going well. I use a simple compass model to navigate these.

My four Ws of performance are Wonderful, Woeful, Wins and Wobbles. These words are deliberately informal and friendly to lower the barrier to use. Imagine how different it would feel if I used success and failure, doubt and achievement. Tone and language matter, and so does our behaviour. How we respond and react to the four Ws sets the tone for our team. Where is your focus now? Where is your default focus? Check your bias; do you only ever talk about wins and wonderful with some people while focusing on wobbles and woe with others?

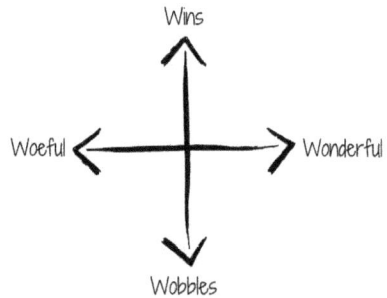

Wins

Woeful — Wonderful

Wobbles

Check your bias.

The way team members are treated when things aren't going well can significantly impact their perceptions of the organisation and flow into your culture. During a crisis, leaders must communicate clearly and transparently, provide support and resources to team members and demonstrate empathy and understanding. This is important whenever team members are experiencing a change, whether it's a change in leadership, policies, or the organisational structure.

Change can be disruptive and unsettling, and how leaders behave and communicate matters. When things aren't going well for an individual, others around them observe and judge how they are managed.

It can be easy to slide into complacency or move quickly to the next piece of work when things are going well. Celebrating success and thanking people for their contribution are two evergreen quick wins. People are watching what you celebrate and how you do so. People notice when you thank others and bring gratitude and a spirit of generosity to play. You don't need a large budget to celebrate or thank people. Constraints drive creativity. Invest time and energy into celebrating wins, no matter how small.

Culture is experienced as a collection of moments.

Of the three groundwork areas, counterintuitively, it's the everyday wins that leaders most often forget.

So, culture is experienced as a collection of moments, and some moments matter more than others. Some moments are also more obvious than others.

These three obvious moments matter in all relationships, not just the workplace. They are the first steps in positive and productive relationships. Children learn about the importance of first impressions when things are going well, and when things are not going well. While we can all do the basics better, this book focuses on the moments that matter that aren't as obvious.

Let's assume you have these three covered and move to the five everyday moments you can action.

Remember, getting the basics right of what you do and how you do it, lays the groundwork for working on your culture.

Getting the basics right lays the groundwork.

Moving into action

At the end of each chapter in Part Two, you'll find a set of experiments to try and some questions to reflect on.

There is no one-size-fits-all approach, so we can't copy and paste ways of working from one organisation to another. What works for one team may not be the right fit for another. The solution is for each team to discover what works for them through experimentation.

Experiments

'Leaders must see themselves as experimenters who lead learning, not dictators who impose control.'

— Peter Scholtes[2]

> Experimenting strengthens your curiosity muscle.

Experimenting strengthens your curiosity muscle. Given that curiosity is one of the core capabilities leaders need to succeed in the coming decades, it's a good one to grow.[3]

I'm not giving you a laundry list of to-do items. Instead, you'll find a menu of experiments to try on for size. Experiments work best when you only have one or two on the go at the same time. This allows you to concentrate on consciously shifting behaviour so you can learn on the way.

Some experiments are for you as the leader. Others will involve a few different people, and many will involve your whole team.

I encourage you to take a deliberate approach when experimenting. Try this five-step deliberate practice approach to optimise your experiments.

Deliberate practice

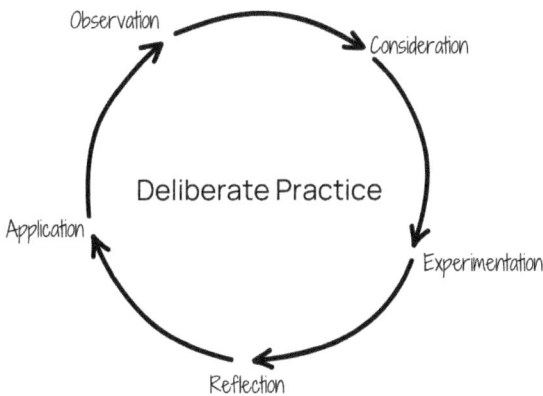

First, **observe**. Before you start changing things, take some time to see how things work now. Then, **consider** what you want to protect and nurture and what you want to tackle first. Consider any risks, issues and opportunities. Now, **experiment**. Some experiments work well if you let the team know upfront. Other experiments work best when you try something and then, like a 1980s radio DJ, back announce what you did and what you learned. After your experiment, **reflect** on what worked, what didn't, and what you'll do differently.

Invite feedback and input from your team. Be comfortable with failing fast and trying something new. Then, **apply** your learning.

Rinse and repeat. The loop starts again: Observation, Consideration, Experimentation, Reflection and Application.

Reflections

*'We do not learn from experience... we
learn from reflecting on experience.'*
— John Dewey [4]

Research shows that reflection is critical to deepening and integrating learning and effectively applying it to our work and our lives. Reflecting on what you have learned can increase your performance by 23%.[5]

Reflection involves reviewing and assessing our assumptions and reactions as well as pondering the meaning and implications. It enables us to move forward in a more considered way.

Use the reflection questions after each chapter as a prompt, but don't be limited by them.

If you don't yet practise reflection, I encourage you to build it into your daily habits. You'll be amazed at how much better you can become through this simple addition to your way of working (and living).

6

Gatherings

Food served family style in the centre of a big table, with everyone helping themselves to what they prefer, works better for me than more formal dining arrangements.

I've always been a people geek. In my twenties, I experimented with hosting social (re)engineering dinners, where I would invite unusual combinations of friends from different backgrounds and life paths. I loved bringing together an eclectic mix of people and watching the wonderful connections and conversations that emerged. Sometimes these were potluck, and sometimes I supplied the food, but everyone knew to bring plenty of drinks and to expect the unexpected when it came to conversation.

As I travelled and lived in Switzerland, Germany, Spain and the UK, I continued to gather and connect people who might not ordinarily meet. As happens when you bring people together without an agenda, conversations meandered. Some were more fun, some more valuable. Over the years, there were certainly many times when we felt like we were solving the problems of the world.

One casual dinner of ten newish parents with seemingly little in common, became friends who met quarterly over a decade of raising children. With professions ranging from health to the arts, mining and financial services to social housing and local government, we would not normally have crossed paths. Naming ourselves the G10, we took turns hosting. Initially, we themed with cuisine and music, which helped add some magic, but we needed this less and less as our relationships deepened. It was fascinating how our experiences mirrored each other, despite not meeting between our get-togethers. Rituals emerged. Conversations were picked up at the next gathering, with some threads continuing over years. Stories were told and retold. Memories were made. Each time we came together, our connections strengthened.

Most of us have hosted gatherings.

Most of us have hosted gatherings. Most of us have attended gatherings and social events. We know what good looks like. And we know when it's not working. So, what happens when we go to work?

The way most organisations gather their people together is fundamentally flawed.

By gatherings, I mean more than online or in-person meetings. Rather, gatherings encompass any time you bring your people together, including social occasions, conferences, learning workshops and even how your hybrid and remote teams come together.

Frustration with meetings is a frequent flyer in my conversations about culture and culture diagnostics. For some organisations, bad meeting culture means that meetings are done poorly. It's the culture *within* the meetings that is the issue. In other organisations, it's overcoming a culture where everyone spends all their days in meetings. Here the issue is a culture *of* meetings.

Why do so few gatherings live up to their potential? How could we shift these from disappointing timewasters to purposeful and productive moments that matter? There is a huge opportunity for leaders to improve connection, engagement and productivity by resetting and reimagining how you and your teams gather. Fix gatherings, and you'll have made significant shifts in your culture.

Come together now

To shift the way we gather, we must change how we work. Traditionally workplaces were filled with synchronous communications. Meetings required everyone to show up, and people were expected to take calls and respond to emails immediately, regardless of what else was happening. Moving to asynchronous communication and ways of working frees up time and capacity to work on what matters most. It allows you to meet on purpose, with purpose. To make the most of when you bring your people together.

> To shift the way we gather, we must change how we work.

What do you think about when you are hosting? When you've invited people over to your place? The notion of host leadership, developed by Mark McKergow, is one of my favourite leadership mindsets. We have all experienced good hosting and good guesting. Most of us recognise it intuitively. We don't have to try too hard to see the similarities between hosting and leading people.

'A host is someone who receives or entertains guests. Hosts sometimes have to act heroically, stepping forward, planning, inviting, introducing, providing. They also act in service – stepping back, encouraging, giving space, joining in.'

— Mark McKergow[1]

I think about checking into a hotel and the difference that someone great at reception makes. It's the difference between a transaction and a welcome. The best welcomes are when you feel expected. I admit to liking the 'welcome back' acknowledgement when I return to a hotel. This is an example of hosting over organising; you feel seen.

It's a good test to run over your calendar. Do you behave as a meeting organiser or a meeting host? Do you behave differently when you are hosting a workplace social gathering? What could you learn from this way of thinking about leading like a host? When it comes to attending meetings, do you behave like a good guest? Pitching in, offering help?

Leadership only works if followership exists. Few of us focus on what it means to be a good follower, but we do know what it means to be a guest. I reckon you can think of a few meetings where your colleagues could have been better guests. Reflect on your own actions and how you could shift to be a better guest when attending someone else's gathering.

Author and facilitator Priya Parker extends the idea of hosting in her book, *The Art of Gathering*. She challenges us to approach meetings and work gatherings with a shift in mindset.

> *'We rely too much on routine and the conventions*
> *of gatherings when we should focus on*
> *distinctiveness and the people involved.'*[2]

Parker reminds us of the importance of purpose, beginnings and endings. Her work, grounded in her experience as a facilitator, stands in contrast to those focused on productivity-led hacks and tactics. She leads with connection and outcomes. This flip provides alternative ways of gathering that have high connection and high impact. Perfect for shifting culture.

Meeting matters

Even before the shift to more hybrid and remote work, I thought a lot about meetings; why, when and how we meet and better ways to meet. Many leaders are frustrated with wasted time, disengaged talent and poorly run meetings. Ask any executive leading a large organisation, and they will tell you that huge swathes of time are lost to meetings. Most organisations have financial delegation policies that limit how much people can spend without approval. Yet if you added up the salary cost of a two-hour meeting, it would usually breach those policies.

So, why do we allow people to book time-wasting meetings when we wouldn't condone the same 'spend' of money?

In 2022 we saw the shift of meeting-free days from smaller tech or creative agencies into the broader domain. An experiment conducted in the UK by Professor Vijay Pereira saw over 1000 organisations adopting meeting-free days and monitored the impact. Introducing just one meeting-free day per week (essentially a 20% reduction in meetings) led to marked increases in productivity, reported as 35%.

Where organisations introduced two meeting-free days per week, productivity increased by a staggering 71%.[3]

Closer to home, Australia's unicorn company, Canva, has set Wednesdays as their organisation-wide meeting-free day, among other new initiatives to support their people's mental health and well-being. The decision to make this organisational shift came from a desire to help their people deal with the fatigue of video calls. Research into communication shifts during the global pandemic found virtual meetings *'tend to be more cognitively demanding, more prone to distraction, and less effective'* than gathering in person.[4]

One of the most commonly asked questions in meetings is, 'Do I really need to be here?' In 2022 research by Steven Rogelberg, team members said they didn't need to be in almost one-third of the meetings they attended.[5] He found employees spend, on average, 18 hours a week in meetings. They only decline 14% of invites even though they'd prefer to back out of 31% of them. Reluctantly going to non-critical meetings wastes about US$25,000 per employee annually. Data from Microsoft's Work Index identified that time spent in meetings has tripled since February 2020, and the number of weekly meetings more than doubled.[6]

A quick shift to make meetings more effective is to reduce the number of people required to attend.

Professor of organisational science, management and psychology, Steven Rogelberg has studied meetings for over 20 years. He shared some compelling findings in his 2018 book, *The Surprising Science of Meetings.*[7] If a meeting starts five minutes late (that only happens in other organisations, right?), it will be 8% less productive. And meetings with more than seven people decrease in effectiveness by 10% for each additional person. To be clear, a meeting with ten people will be 30% less effective than a meeting with seven people.

I love Priya Parker's recommendation to 'exclude generously'.[8] Being deliberate about who you invite is vital to sustainable and productive meetings. I would add 'include graciously'. Not to expand your invitation list but rather to think about what value they will gain, not just what they will bring.

Bill Ash, the author of *Redesigning Conversations,*[9] asks us to consider 'Is this meeting conducive for all?' As gracious hosts, we would consider the needs of those gathering and anticipate what is required. Once underway, we would continue to monitor and actively include guests. In a workplace context, gracious inclusion involves more effort into actively including without feeling like we are overdoing it (which sometimes leads to resentment or exhaustion of goodwill).

The best meetings are held *on* purpose, *with* purpose. Whether small over a coffee or in a large conference, the meeting leader's role is to provide clarity and connection. Collaboration and collective problem-solving are best when we're together in a room. But there are countless ways to work collaboratively to solve problems that don't involve being in a room. There are good reasons to bring people together. Don't choose the meeting format as your default. Like all habits, it is worth noticing your own defaults and challenging yourself to look for the best option. If you do choose to gather your people, do it on purpose, with a clear purpose.

> The best meetings are held *on* purpose, *with* purpose.

Author and organisational psychologist Adam Grant says there are four reasons to meet 'to decide, learn, bond and do. If it doesn't serve one of those purposes, cancel it.'[10] A clear purpose for the meeting goes a long way toward improving the quality of the experience and the outcomes.

Keep meetings small, short and focused. And try meeting standing up. It will change your life. Research shows sit-down meetings last 34% longer than stand-up meetings.[11] Bob Sutton, professor of organisational behaviour at Stanford University, looked at the research on group size and concluded the most productive meetings contain only five to eight people. Why? The quality of conversation begins to erode, as does preparation, participation and action.[12]

Lazy hybrid is even worse than lazy in-person or lazy online meetings. As Bryan Whitefield, an expert in risk, influence and decision-making, says, 'Hybrid rarely works unless very well thought through and cultural norms ensure online participants are "present".' He often advises leaders and risk specialists on facilitating risk workshops. Bryan's model of Invaluable Conversations is a great example of culture in the room impacting outcomes. He says two things are needed for invaluable conversations — a trusting environment and true insights into the decisions that need to be made by the team. As the diagram shows, if you cannot do either, the conversations are meaningless and the results are nonsense. If you achieve one and not the other, you either have pleasant conversations in a trust-only environment or awkward ones when insights are delivered without trust. Both are a form of lost opportunity.[13]

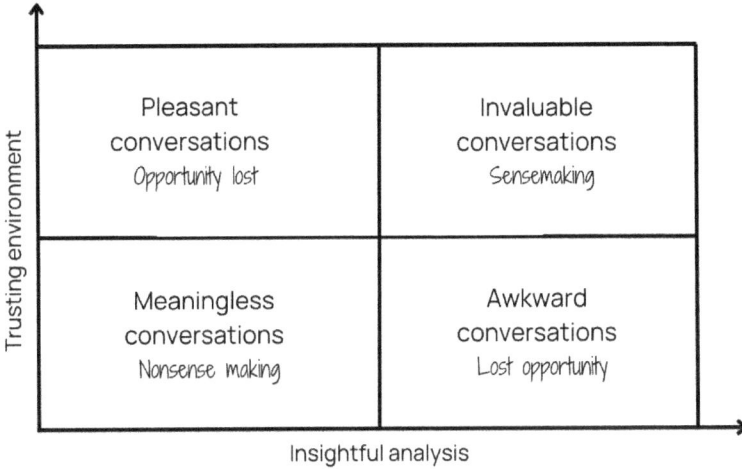

Invaluable Conversations, Bryan Whitefield

There are thousands of resources to help you host better meetings and a similar number on how to contribute better when you're in them. In addition to Steven Rogelberg's book, *The Surprising Science of Meetings,* I highly recommend Priya Parker's *The Art of Gathering* published in 2018.

We've collectively learned to shift from zero to hero using online meeting technology, but if you'd like to dig into hybrid and remote gatherings, explore the work of Gustavo Razzetti in *Remote Not Distant*[14] and David Burkus in *Leading From Anywhere.*[15] If you want to boost levels of connection in your gatherings, access anything from Chad Littlefield on YouTube.[16]

Individually you can improve your meetings by utilising the time together better, hosting and attending fewer meetings. However, it takes a collective effort to shift the culture of meetings. Invite your team to design better meetings. Inspire a movement to collectively fix meetings.

You've wasted enough time and energy. You have some decisions to make. You can keep complaining that you waste too much time in meetings or start doing the work to make them worthwhile. You can subject your direct reports to death by PowerPoint or provide clarity and engage them with humour and storytelling. It's time for you to shift gears as a leader. It's time to shift how you gather your people.

Getting away

I spend more time than most at retreats, offsites and conferences. As a facilitator and speaker, I work with leadership teams when they are out of their day-to-day environment and focused on their reason for gathering. Whether facilitating a weeklong retreat, delivering a keynote or masterclass, I have the privilege and opportunity to see the team out of the building.

Taking time *away* from the business to work *on* the business applies to culture work too. Stepping out of the culture to work on the culture fosters perspective, focus and an intensity that is challenging to achieve in a 90-minute session on the agenda of a full-day leadership team meeting.

For every day I deliver, I spend at least two designing and planning the experience. While you might not need to achieve the same ratio, the ROI (Return on Investment) for design and planning, part of the value of taking everyone away is ramping up the investment in thought and care that goes into the gathering. We spend more time focusing on making the gathering worth the effort. Cultures that work are more deliberate about the 'worth it' factor.

While I believe culture is best shifted in everyday moments, bringing people together can act as a culture shift accelerant. Key to this approach is a culture incubator, where we gather a selection of the best and brightest to co-create and incubate the chosen culture of the organisation. We draw people from a diagonal slice across the organisation so that every area and level is represented. The nomination list is a carefully balanced mix of tenure, profession, gender, generation, location and nationality. The experience of the incubator is heavily designed and curated to rapidly build trust and a shared understanding of culture and each other. From this platform, we co-create the desired culture and a range of assets to support the culture shift.

Cultures that work host effective and impactful gatherings because they understand experience matters. Leaders are more deliberate. They do more by design and less by default. When gathering their people, they consider the who, what, how, when, where and why.

> Do more by design and less by default.

It matters who attends, so be deliberate about who is included and excluded. The content (the what) of the session matters. Be considered about the agenda, or if you're meeting without agenda, determine your process. Match how you come together with the desired outcomes. Use the name of the meeting to offer clues about what to expect and how to behave. We show up differently to a brainstorm than a rumble. We prepare differently for a board meeting than for a team work-in-progress session.

The time of day matters. Many organisations have shifted their regular team meetings to be held on a flexible schedule or at more family-friendly times. If the content is more conversational or creative, plan for an afternoon timeslot. If you need detailed or complex thinking, schedule a morning session. Consider the time zones of attendees and allow notice and travel time for in-person sessions.

Location matters. Our choices are more than the binary in-person or online. Choose a fit-for-purpose venue, or resources, such as online collaboration tools, to match the participants, process and outcomes. For special occasions, consider an aspirational venue to inspire and delight. Make attending worth it.

Flexibility matters. There is no one great way to gather that will suit all in your organisation. One of my clients has introduced WOW kits, where templates and conversation cards have been developed to assist leaders and teams in designing their own ways of working. The kits outline multiple options and ideas covering meeting cadence, location, content and protocols.

> ## What differentiates good from great gatherings? Meaning.

What matters most, what differentiates good from great gatherings, is meaning. Meaning is often linked, but not always, to purpose. Sure, achieving the objective of the gathering feels better than missing it or wasting time. Yet gatherings that create meaning live in people's memories long after effective meetings are forgotten.

Connection and contribution

Two vital ingredients for gatherings in cultures that work are belonging and psychological safety.

We don't think of community and belonging as something to learn, but in Denmark, it is a fundamental part of education from when children are very young. An analysis of over 300,000 participants in a 2016 Danish Prosperity Survey showed that a high level of *fællesskab* (togetherness) positively affected every facet of well-being: from school drive to improved learning, to better involvement, competence levels, and increased peace of mind.

The Danes focus on *trivsel* (thriving) from early childhood learning onward. One of the most important standardised tests all students and teachers take each year across Denmark is the *trivsel* test. The questions are similar to workplace psychological safety assessments, such as 'Do you feel seen and heard?', 'Would you help a classmate if they were upset?' The Danes believe that academic ability will follow when well-being is sound. If only we adhered to this in the workplace.

A longing for belonging

If we put our anthropological caps on, belonging has roots in biological protection, physical safety, and security. In prehistoric times, belonging was linked to survival. Many cultures used exclusion and casting out as the height of punishment. We want to belong so we are not left alone or behind.

We want to belong.

I think belonging is the destination of all diversity, equity and inclusion work. When people feel they belong, they can bring their personal best and bring out the best in others. That's the kind of culture people want to work in.

True belonging requires authenticity and vulnerability. As a leader, modelling authenticity and vulnerability gives permission to those around you to show up that way. Author and professor

Brené Brown's work on trust, vulnerability and courage talks about belonging and fitting in. If you haven't created a culture where people can be vulnerable, then trust will always be constrained. Trust is necessary for great teamwork; it is the differentiator for sustainable outperformance. Belonging is a game changer. Brené's differentiation of these two concepts helps us better understand them and their implications when gathering teams.

'If I get to be me, I belong. If I have to be like you, I fit in.'[17]

When bringing people together, some people will feel vulnerable or threatened. Social pressures or concerns can be exacerbated in the workplace. If your people don't feel like they belong, gatherings will see people 'performing' and showing up how they think they need to show up to be successful. Others will be striving to fit in. For those with a low sense of belonging and safety, the constant threat assessment will limit their cognitive ability and starve their contribution. When people are focused more on how they show up than how they are contributing or leading, the value of the gathering is reduced. In some cultures, I've seen behaviour that was so performative that I felt like I should have bought a ticket.

McKinsey's research into the 'Great Attrition' highlighted that more than 50% of employees who had left their job in the six months prior, lacked a sense of belonging.[18] One Harvard study found that 61% of employees 'feel pressure to cover some facet of their identity at work'.[19]

A 2019 study by BetterUp found that workplace belonging can lead to an estimated 56% increase in job performance, a 50% reduction in turnover risk, and a 75% decrease in employee sick days. The study found that a single incidence of 'micro-exclusion' can lead to an immediate 25% decline in an individual's performance on a team project.[20]

The good news is that our brains are wired for connection, helping us create meaningful bonds. However, how we build and lead teams can activate those brain structures for either trust and collaboration or conflict and competition.

Cultures that work focus on fostering trust, collaboration, inclusion and social connections. If your team members feel like they belong and have a sense of worthiness, they feel psychologically safe. If they don't, they feel overlooked, undervalued and unsafe. Cultures that work are psychologically safe.

> Cultures that work focus on fostering trust.

Psychological safety is a term that refers to feeling confident that you will not be rejected or punished for speaking up in a group setting. The term was coined by Harvard University professor Dr Amy Edmondson and explored in her book, *The Fearless Organisation*.[21]

In 2004, she analysed two hospitals and noted that teams that reported the fewest errors were not necessarily the best performing. If you also factored in lawsuits, patient recovery and insurance claims, teams with the fewest errors didn't do so well. Teams with the fewest reported errors typically were mired in a high-blame team culture. While the reported number of errors was low, lawsuits, patient recovery and insurance claims suggested otherwise. Teams that exhibited traits of a just culture and psychological safety had a higher error count. But openness allowed team members to learn from mistakes, resulting in fewer lawsuits, insurance claims, and better patient recovery over time.

For psychological safety to be present, the group members must have a shared belief that it is safe to take interpersonal risks. That means people trust and respect each other within the group.

Psychological safety is not about being liked or protected from uncomfortable opinions or beliefs. Instead, it is about feeling confident that you can openly share your thoughts and feedback without fear of repercussions. Google's well-known study, the Aristotle Project, sought to determine what separates the best teams from average and poor ones.[22] They looked at many factors and found that psychological safety was more important than anything else — even whether the team members were good at their jobs. The best teams showed empathy towards each other and actively sought out everyone's contributions, not just those of a few.

If your meeting culture isn't driving connection and contribution, you have work to do. No amount of focusing on agendas and meeting technology will improve performance if you don't have a basis of psychological safety in teams and a sense of belonging and connection with individuals.

We need to shift the way we work and bring people together on purpose with purpose.

Remember, how and why we gather matters more than an agenda or meeting technology.

Experiments

Introduce a meeting-free day across the organisation. If it takes too long to navigate this, start smaller or start local. Demonstrate the possibility. Create a ripple of envy across your organisation. Monitor results and report on key metrics so you can showcase the benefits.

Reset. Cancel all meetings and reset your calendar. Slowly reintroduce meetings. Use seasonal rhythm to your advantage. Conduct a spring clean. Use the 'NO' energy in November to end date all meetings in December so you can start your new year afresh. Use the 'new year, new me' momentum in January or July (or whenever your financial year starts) to delete the old and dated things in your calendar and set up new fresh invitations.

Don't set and forget. Pay special attention to recurring meetings. Don't set recurring meetings for more than three months and review at the 12-week mark. Don't leave bad habits in your diary. Work through all recurring meetings in your calendar and ensure they have an end date. Never set up a meeting without an end date.

Get out of the building. Look for opportunities to meet and gather with your people in different locations. Location matters — whether it's coffee, a walking meeting for your one-on-ones, or a quarterly offsite. A different perspective awaits.

Host with the most. Shift your mindset from meeting organiser to leader as host. What would change? What would you care about when you're a host that is different to being an organiser?

Check in. I always start meetings with an informal check-in. They are a quick and simple hack to build psychological safety. A simple round of people sharing how they are or something they did on the weekend shifts the mood in the meeting. If you have been using these for a while and are looking for new inspiration to re-energise this process with your team, try some online auto generators, such as https://thedigitalworkplace.com/checkin/ or https://checkin.daresay.io/ for new check-in (and check-out) prompts.

Reflections

How are you bringing your people together?

How many meetings do you attend that have a clear purpose?

How many meetings do you attend that involve more than seven people? Who could be generously excluded?

How can you be more deliberate about the meetings you host and attend?

What opportunities do you have today to improve the psychological safety of your team?

Rituals

Rituals create a space

For an American, Emma Gibbens is pretty passionate about Acknowledgements of Country. Emma and her good friend and business partner, Rhys Paddick, work with Australians to lose the script and move beyond tokenism to find a sense of connection to each other, Country and culture by crafting a more authentic Acknowledgement of Country.

Emma is a change strategist and experienced facilitator. Rhys is an Aboriginal educator who describes his work as cultural de-sensitisation. Together, they founded Acknowledge This to teach people the concepts behind the words when delivering an Acknowledgement of Country.[1]

When I chatted with Rhys and Emma about the power of culture, ritual and storytelling, we found lots of common ground. Emma says:

'Acknowledgements of Country are a ritualised practice of connection at the beginning of every meeting. It's almost a suspended space, separate from the rest of your

work culture, where you can bring more vulnerability,
more openness, more personal storytelling.[2]

Rhys explores the rituals of greeting someone when he meets them for the first time. He says in Western business culture, we shake hands and ask how things are. We may chat about the weather. We move fairly quickly to share our roles and usually reference our job titles. We identify by what we do. When Rhys meets with Aboriginal people, the ritual is back to front. The greeting starts with where you are from. The first question is about your mob.

'Tell me who you are related to or who you know.
The focus is on the individual and the community
and how I connect to you, rather than the role
or job title you hold or the work you do. [3]

Rhys believes that rituals remind us of our social nature. Regardless of the ritual itself, sitting down for coffee, shaking hands or hugs are all agreements to participate together in a culture.

Deeper into our conversation, Rhys and Emma spoke about the power of rituals to level power dynamics. Acknowledgements of Country are a relatively recent tradition in corporate Australia and have become a box-ticking exercise in some organisations. Unfortunately, in these organisations, acknowledgements have been locked down and scripted to remove any risk of offence. Doing so also erases any personal connection.

Emma and Rhys shared how one of their clients has moved well beyond scripts, adopting an open approach to acknowledgements. This major health organisation in Western Australia starts meetings with a space, asking who is feeling called to acknowledge today. They allow a five to ten-minute space at the start of the meeting. No one is assigned to speak; anyone can share their acknowledgement. This approach reinforces the flat power dynamics of their culture while creating a safe place for authentic Acknowledgments of Country to be heard.

This is the power of ritual at play.

Rituals carry culture

Rituals create space for your team to come together. In *Humour Seriously,* Jennifer Aaker and Naomi Bagdonas describe rituals as cultural carriers that influence people's behaviours by tapping into their emotions.[4] They shift cultures one nudge at a time.

Often, the norms and unwritten rules of culture are demonstrated through rituals. Rituals are collective behaviours that are repeated, shared and learned. Together, they build and strengthen connections among team members and convey your culture. They may be visible through your welcoming and onboarding activities, how you gather and meet, celebrate and reward team members, and how you make decisions and resolve conflicts.

Rituals enrich and reinforce cultures. There remains plenty of scope and opportunity for organisations to use them better to shift or strengthen their culture.

> Rituals enrich and reinforce cultures.

Rituals enrich culture

How do you celebrate your birthday? Does it involve cake? Do you make a wish when you blow out the candles? While examples of rituals vary, nearly all human societies celebrate birthdays.

Like language, rituals exist in all cultures. They create community and build and cement a sense of belonging.

Let's consider your birthday at work. Perhaps you take your birthday off work each year? In the workplace, do you arrive to a decorated desk? Are you expected to bring a cake? Or do you celebrate all the August birthdays at a combined morning tea and the executive assistant organises a cake? Or perhaps it's your shout for team drinks? Does an envelope, or PayPal link, travel around the team collecting contributions toward a gift?

> Defn. — A ritual is a conscious set of
> actions, or patterns of behaviour, that
> are performed in a particular order or
> way, with symbolic meaning.

The easiest way to identify a ritual is to assess whether an otherwise ordinary task has meaning and symbolism. For example, it isn't a ritual if you light a candle when the lights go out in a storm. Yet turning off the lights and lighting a candle for your bath is.

Let's look at a few more aspects of rituals to help you identify them in your culture.

A ritual is not a habit. Habits are unconscious patterns of behaviour, while rituals are deliberate. You may not think of birthday cakes as rituals because they are familiar, but organising a cake to celebrate is a deliberate and conscious decision.

A ritual is not a routine. While routines are what we repeatedly do, rituals also foster meaning. Rituals can happen every day, once a week or annually, depending on the trigger. Repeating an activity doesn't make it a ritual. It is the sense of meaning created that elevates a routine to ritual. Saying hello every morning is not a ritual in itself. You can, however, design your morning greeting ritual to be memorable and impactful.

Rituals are triggers. Often a ritual signals a transition. You can frame your day or your week with start and end-of-day rituals. Consciously or not, many of us have Monday morning and Friday evening rituals. Rituals can signal a shift from one state to another. They can ground you and help you feel ready for what is ahead. In teams, rituals help align the team's state and smooth transitions.

> # Rituals can signal a shift.

Rituals are triggered. Triggers are typically a time or an event, for example, starting the working week with a Monday morning coffee or ending the financial year with a team lunch. Event ritual triggers include someone joining or leaving the team. Often significant life events trigger workplace rituals such as getting married or becoming a parent.

Rituals are more than an event. Both events and rituals occur with a particular frequency or at a certain time, but meaning elevates an event to a ritual.

Rituals can be rewards and rewards can be ritualised. The key to something being a ritual is the emotional payoff or reward resulting from the ritual.

Purpose and power

Rituals are purposeful and powerful, not random or transactional. Rituals often have a rhythm and a reason. They can be a tool that brings a stronger sense of personal meaning and belonging to an organisation. Rituals are like a pre-verbal language read by our senses and intuition. In many situations, they help us to embody our belief systems. Rituals activate nostalgia, a powerful psychological response that maintains and enhances meaning by connecting the present with the past.

The strength of rituals is their ability to contribute to a sense of identity, belonging and cohesion among teams. Rituals help to create a sense of belonging and cohesion among team members by providing a shared experience to bond over. This can lead to feelings of camaraderie and connection among team members. Rituals often create memories that team members will remember for a long time, perhaps a special event, a team-building activity, or a recognition ceremony. These memories can evoke positive emotions and create a sense of nostalgia. That is the stuff that stories are made of.

Rituals also help create a sense of purpose and meaning for team members, improving motivation and engagement. They can also communicate and reinforce the purpose and priorities of your organisation.

Focusing on something greater than ourselves also decreases stress and anxiety. Rituals establish routines and predictability in the workplace, providing team members with a sense of security and comfort. As the world becomes more uncertain, this kind of certainty can help people cope better.

Rituals ground us. The stress hormone cortisol is lower and oxytocin levels are greater when we practice rituals.[5] We feel better, safer and more connected.[6] The same occurs in teams.

Professor Kevin Kniffin is a Cornell University organisational psychologist. His father was a firefighter, so he grew up around them. Kniffin's research into what makes some teams more productive than others centred on firefighters. His work highlighted the power of teams making meals and eating together. The relationships formed and strengthened around the dining table were key to reducing stress and building trust.[7]

Rituals communicate and reinforce what matters most in your organisation. Rituals are non-verbal ways of communicating what's important. Whatever language you use – purpose, values, principles – all are ways to share your culture verbally. Attaching rituals to these can enhance the associated meaning and make the words on the poster come alive. Rituals can strengthen the sense of connection to your vision, strategy and objectives. This can lead to feelings of alignment and connection to the organisation.

Some rituals continue from long-standing traditions and can evoke emotional connection due to their historical significance. People value annual events that have occurred for decades or a ritual passed down from previous generations. Positive traditions nurture loyalty, especially those linked to your origin story.

In this era of hyper-personalisation, supercharge your rituals by personalising them to reflect your team members' interests, beliefs, or culture. This can help to create a sense of emotional connection to the ritual and your organisation.

Workplace rituals evoke emotional connections and responses by creating a sense of belonging, providing a sense of purpose, and emphasising what matters most to the organisation. Rituals contribute to team cohesion and performance, often symbolically reinforcing what

Supercharge your rituals by personalising them.

matters most in your culture. They have a 'pull' effect through the participation of team members, connecting them with the culture. Canadian neurologist Donald Calne wrote, 'Reason leads to conclusions. Emotion leads to action.'[8] That is the heart of why rituals are so powerful when it comes to cultures that work.

Rituals at work

Rituals play a significant role in shaping culture, values and norms. Many organisations have implemented unique and effective rituals as part of their culture, contributing to their success and reputation. Here are examples of well-known organisations that have done just that.

Google is renowned for its innovative and unique approach to workplace culture, which includes a variety of rituals. One of the most well-known is the TGIF (Thank God It's Friday) all-hands meeting, where team members gather to hear updates from the organisation's leadership team and ask questions. This ritual promotes transparency and open communication and helps to foster a sense of community among team members.

3M, the multinational conglomerate, has a long-standing tradition of 15% time, where team members are encouraged to spend 15% of their workweek pursuing personal projects and interests. This ritual promotes innovation and is influential in attracting talent to 3M.

Rio Tinto starts each meeting with a safety share, a ritual practised across many mining and manufacturing organisations. People gather to share stories about safety, typically based on their own experiences or observations. It ensures everyone focuses on safety and how their behaviours contribute to it. At Rio Tinto, each team member is asked to sign a personal safety commitment to act safely and put safety first — at work and at home.

Zappos, the online shoe and clothing retailer, is recognised for its unique and quirky culture, which includes a variety of rituals. One of the most well-known is Fun Fridays, where team members are encouraged to wear costumes and participate in fun activities. This ritual helps to promote creativity and a positive work-life balance and fosters a sense of community among team members.

Ritualising success

We often use rituals to celebrate successes and milestones. When things are going well, celebrations provide time to pause and reflect, which offers neurological and social benefits.[9] When reviewing cultures for organisations, I often find they don't take time to celebrate. Sharing and celebrating what good looks like allows others to see what your organisation values. How you celebrate, signals what is important. They are cultural moments of truth.

> Celebrations provide time to pause and reflect.

You may have seen or heard bells ringing when sales are made or high fives after a win. Maybe your team has a victory dance. It's amazing how quickly you can shift the vibe by playing music, and dancing adds to the energy. You've also likely seen boring, anaemic Team Member of the Month awards that are undervalued and even avoided.

An experienced retail executive, Antony Moore, reflected on organisations he'd worked with where the Employee of the Month scheme was almost weaponised. The award had to be made, even when there were no worthy winners. Team members worked this out fairly quickly and the program became quite toxic.

Moore says things are quite different where he now works at The Lottery Corporation. 'We celebrate success each week in our team meetings and have a Teams chat page for successes. We celebrate lengths of service and birthdays weekly at our team updates and have monthly get-togethers, usually involving food of some kind, with a theme to facilitate local connections for teams within our team. We also celebrate success in our weekly digital newsletters.' He believes consistency is key. Doing things here and there doesn't reinforce the right culture.

Rewards can be ritualised. The art of presenting a trophy to someone shapes how the trophy will be valued. If you diminish or undermine the Team Member of the Month award, it will move from motivating to demotivating. The reverence given to the trophy or artefact accentuates the meaning of the ritual. Whether it's top of the leader board, MVP (Most Valued Player), greatest effort or the most spectacular failure, rewards signal what is valued. Highly prized awards don't always have to be for the best at anything. Reinforcing what matters most means you will likely get more of it. As the adage goes, you get what you pay for.

When we take a broader view of success beyond purely winning, we expand opportunities for our teams to find purpose and fulfilment in their work. Rituals provide a way to understand what matters in our organisation and a mechanism to promote and recognise different kinds of success. I always look for how tenure is acknowledged or celebrated in organisations as a data point. I've found a high correlation between organisations that revere experience and their celebration of loyalty.

Rituals don't need a crowd; they can be solo affairs. Sometimes the most powerful thing you can do as a leader is to role-model your own rituals and create space for others to do so too. I encourage the leaders I work with to practise gratitude

Rituals don't need a crowd.

and to promote the practice in their teams. Just one person kicking the morning off in the team chat with something they are grateful for can have a flow-on effect.

When things aren't going well

Rituals can provide a sense of accomplishment and positivity during challenging times. Celebrations and ceremonies help to lift team member morale and create a sense of shared success, even when things are hard. If celebrating is inappropriate, a muted gathering acknowledging achievements or efforts is still worth going ahead with. In these situations, pay more attention to the surrounding messaging and signals you want to send.

In times of need, rituals can provide comfort and stability for your teams. During uncertainty or stress, they create predictability. And during change, regular team meetings or check-ins can help team members feel more connected and informed. In the event of a loss or tragedy, a moment's silence can help teammates process their emotions and honour the memory of a colleague, offering closure and support. When things are challenging, rituals emphasise community.

Rituals connect team members with the organisation's purpose. Feeling like they are making a difference and contributing to something bigger than themselves helps team members focus on the positives when things are tough.

Rituals connect team members with the organisation's purpose.

The brain's ability to operate on auto-pilot kicks in when we experience a familiar ritual, as it quietens our minds, reduces anxiety and brings us back to focus. Sometimes during a crisis, when people aren't fully occupied, rituals allow them to focus on achieving something together. For those intensely involved in responding, breaking for a ritual can provide relief and time to focus on the simple and familiar.

Rituals provide a socially acceptable behavioural nudge when feedback may not.

As a non-beer drinker, I was struck by how often something was deemed a 'carton offence' on mine sites. Whether you were contributing a carton to the next crew barbecue or the Christmas party, infractions ranged from being late to a meeting or getting a vehicle bogged. The team cheerfully assigned penalties and banter was shared freely.

The ritual of being called out to buy the carton allowed teams to nudge behaviour that wasn't appropriate without alienating the recipient. The act of buying and sharing a carton with teammates provided a path of penance with social acceptance. My (highly scientific) research approach utilising LinkedIn received a long list of infractions deemed carton-worthy and prompted the insight that this was more prevalent in male-dominated industries.

Ritualising failure

While some brave cultures embrace 'safe to fail' as a mantra, it's been problematic for others to accept this as a guiding principle. Atlassian's shift from 'fail fast' to 'fail well' is probably more palatable. If you're going to fail, make it count.

Nelson Mandela comes to mind with his approach of playing to win or playing to learn.

Cultures that work learn from failure. They encourage experimentation, vulnerability and learning. When a failure happens, reviewing and sharing the learning means we are better placed for next time. Focusing on learning limits blame and shame and builds psychological safety. That means people feel safe to share ideas and be vulnerable, which are necessary ingredients for innovation. Mechanisms to review and debrief failures aren't always conducive to learning, even with psychological safety. Ritualising how you uncover and share the learning linked to failures can certainly make the process less risky. The opportunity is to use rituals to supercharge learning, contributing to a culture where people and teams can fail well.

> Use rituals to supercharge learning.

Rita McGrath refers to 'intelligent failure' as where lessons are shared across the whole organisation. Her Harvard Business Review article, *Failing by Design*, discusses the importance of having a graceful way to exit and shut down initiatives.[10] Rituals can reinforce each step along the way and provide meaning and a sense of broader continuity, even when a project is folding.

Welcomes and farewells

Welcomes and farewells are fertile ground for rituals in cultures around the world. They are also a great place to start as a leader seeking to understand more about workplace rituals.

Hello and welcome

Welcomes matter, whether it's how you greet people each morning or how you welcome new people into your team. The next time you enter your workplace, take note of the welcoming rituals of different people and teams. Observe how and when welcomes occur throughout the day. Think about how you would like to be greeted in different situations, then act accordingly.

Early in my leadership career, I received feedback that I only greeted *my* team when I walked onto the floor. The surrounding teams felt slighted that I didn't acknowledge them, which led them to think that I didn't believe they or their work mattered. Of course, this was never my intent.

I'm incredibly grateful to that team's supervisor, Cathy, for pulling me aside to give me that feedback. I was horrified, but it was simple to fix. By shifting my good morning greeting to include all the teams, I was able to smooth the concerns and build better relationships. The flow on impact was that relationships between my team and the others also improved. It's more than 15 years since I received that feedback, but it has stayed with me. I've been more deliberate about greetings and welcomes ever since.

I often share the story of the impact a group of student nurses had on their workplace purely by smiling and saying hello. I first read this story on https://www.whattheheckisarbejdsglaede.com/.[11] Arbejdsglaede is a Danish word for happiness at work.

The four newly graduated nurses started their first jobs together on a children's ward. They were shocked and dismayed to find themselves in an unhappy work environment with high levels of dissatisfaction and low collaboration. Gossip and complaints dominated the conversations taking place. The four young nurses decided to take action. In addition to creating a simple recognition scheme where colleagues praised each other, they started smiling and greeting everyone they interacted with. It took six months for the workplace to turn around. Happiness and satisfaction levels increased for the medical workforce and also for the young patients and their families. All from shifting to greeting every person on the ward with a smile.

Marriott International teach all new starters to smile and greet every guest. They use the 15/5 rule in their brand standards to guide their associates globally. Any guest within 5 feet should be greeted verbally and with a smile, and any guest within 15 feet should be met with eye contact, a friendly nod or some other gesture.

It's a good guideline for leaders to keep in mind. How often do you walk through your workplace looking at your phone? Shifting your behaviour to make eye contact with people in the area and greeting them as you walk past will have a small but noticeable impact on the culture. Role modelling greetings and setting expectations for your leaders to do the same will have a ripple effect on how welcoming your culture is.

Onboarding

How you welcome new starters introduces your culture, purpose and priorities and sets the scene for success. Investing in your onboarding approach will pay dividends. Design onboarding rituals that contribute positively to the experience and elevate your onboarding from a compliance process to an experience. No single onboarding formula will work for all organisations or individuals, but using rituals will enrich the experience.

Adam Taylor is the founder of the Custom Learning Collective.[12] He believes a great onboarding experience is more than an induction, compliance modules, orientation and assigning a buddy. To set an organisation apart, he emphasises the importance of personal and human-oriented rituals that are leader-led.

To create an exceptional onboarding experience, Adam recommends implementing several practices. Firstly, immediately after the recruiter has sealed the deal or confirmed the employment offer, call the new hire to congratulate them on their new role. Secondly, send an email before the new starter's first day introducing each team member with a photo, their position, and a personal titbit, such as their favourite food or song. This assists in making the new hire feel more welcomed and familiar with their new colleagues.

Additionally, Adam suggests starting the new team member on a day other than Monday, since the first day of the week tends to be busy. Starting on a different day gives more time for onboarding and ensures people are available to assist the new hire. Importantly, he says, objectives should be set from day one. It is powerful to create a task for the new person to complete by the end of the first week and another by the end of the first month, followed by regular check-ins to ensure they are on track.

To welcome the new team member to the team, try organising a team lunch on their first day, preferably in person, to facilitate team bonding. Ideally, in their first month, create a new team charter or agreement with the involvement of the whole team. This process should be a fresh agreement, not merely an update of the old one, since a new team member changes the team's dynamics.

A welcome that's hard to ignore

The New Zealand rugby All Blacks' legendary haka creates a famous first impression. Imagine being welcomed to your next critical negotiation with a haka. Many people think this traditional pre-game ritual is performed so the team can intimidate their enemies — and they are right. But beyond this, the All Blacks use the haka to 'reconnect with their fundamental purpose, to connect to the core of their culture, to summon their ancestors up from the earth and to bond with one another.'[13] The All Blacks' haka conveys ferocity and connection to their teammates and heritage.

It is a passionate, traditional Māori war dance or challenge that was historically used on the battlefield to prepare warriors mentally and physically for battle. Less well-known is that the ritual was also performed when groups came together in peace. It is a celebration of life. Research shows that rituals trigger feelings of connection, timelessness and meaning. These feelings stimulate a state of mental flow. Of course, few organisations use stylised physical rituals such as the haka.

The All Blacks have harnessed the power of rituals besides the haka. James Kerr's book *Legacy* highlights the All Blacks' ritual of 'sweeping the sheds'. Cleaning the locker room before they leave demonstrates both personal discipline and humility. As Kerr writes:

> *'Sweeping the sheds. Doing it properly. So no one*
> *else has to. Because no one looks after the All*
> *Blacks. The All Blacks look after themselves.'*[14]

Farewells

In culture incubators, I often poll the group on whether people wave goodbye at the end of Zoom meetings. Does this occur in your workplace? If it doesn't, and you are meeting online with people from outside your organisation, it really stands out when the rituals differ as you farewell people. It's an excellent example of the simple rituals we engage in without conscious thought.

When someone leaves their job at an Apple store, regardless of whether they were promoted or are leaving the organisation, their colleagues stop what they are doing and applaud them as they leave the store. They hug, high five and say thank you. It's an honour guard of sorts.

A test of your culture is how well you treat people when they leave an organisation. Great leaders know their role is to develop potential into talent and that there will come a time when that talent will move on. Cultures that over-index loyalty or create a strong 'we' feeling by casting others down, sometimes punish people when they resign.

Of course, there are better and worse ways to resign, but assuming positive intent, celebrating farewells provides an opportunity to honour and thank someone for their contribution. Current team members take note of how leavers are treated. A positive, respectful experience on the way out is more likely to create a revolving door where alumni talent will wish to return to your organisation. The recency effect applies too; your previously engaged team member now vividly remembers how they were treated and shares that with potential talent. Stories will be told – what do you want them to be?

Change your rituals, change your culture

Rituals provide a focal point when shifting culture. Leaders can signal shifts in what matters to the organisation by deliberately stopping, reshaping, or designing new rituals. As rituals don't typically require a significant investment, they can be a visible, quick win. People notice shifts in rituals, particularly in times of change.

> People notice shifts in rituals.

Changing rituals can signal changes in culture

Outdated rituals can negatively impact morale and productivity, while adapting to change and creating new rituals can help organisations stay aligned with their purpose and strategy. A regular review ensures that rituals meet their intended purpose and resonate with team members. By changing your rituals, you can change your culture for the better.

The introduction of a single meaningful and widespread ritual can be a powerful signal that your organisation has shifted priorities. Increasing the focus on Corporate Social Responsibility could mean you create a new ritual of monthly volunteer opportunities for team members. Introducing the Acknowledgement of Country at every gathering would signal a greater focus on respect and reconciliation for indigenous Australians. The attendance of the chief customer officer at all team inductions could highlight the shift to customer centricity.

Refresh your rituals to sustain their impact. Over time, certain rituals may become outdated and no longer align with what matters most to the organisation. For example, a traditional annual organisation-wide conference may no longer effectively communicate important information to team members. With the rise of technology and virtual platforms and the increasing pace of change, more frequent virtual townhalls may be more effective.

You might need to change the format of a ritual to suit your team members' needs better. Where a ritual is highly valued but no longer relevant, try respectfully moving it to your historical context and replace it with something more aligned with today's workplace. For example, black and white photos on a history wall commemorate the annual Christmas drinks event, which is now updated to an end-of-financial-year family day. Outdated rituals can lead to a disconnect between team members and the organisation, negatively impacting morale and productivity.

Outdated rituals can lead to a disconnect.

Rituals are valuable and often undervalued. Most don't carry a cost, yet deliver a high rate of return. The investment required is time, energy and focus. Rituals help leaders increase psychological safety and belonging.[15] They improve connection,[16] cohesion, alignment,[17] productivity and engagement while reducing anxiety[18] and stress.[19] It is worth investing in the design and use of rituals in your teams.

Now we understand what rituals are and why they are essential, it's time for action.

Map your rituals

Consider the rituals in your team today. Have some become meaningless? Are they missing the mark? Are you losing out on opportunities to ritualise routines or rewards? Is it time to review and design rituals for your team to shape your chosen culture?

Conduct an audit. Use triggers or events to identify what rituals are currently practised in your team. Start with beginnings and endings. Think about celebrations, commiserations and rewards. Add in how you mark occasions such as life events or cyclical business occasions.

Examine your personal rituals and how they contribute to your performance. Apply the same process.

Design your own ritual

While rituals from other organisations can inspire you, it's important to design your own.

You can't force a ritual — it must be authentic. While unique practices can be remarkable and contribute to your culture being known and celebrated, don't die on the hill of terminal uniqueness. Don't over-engineer them. Rituals work best when they are simple and human.

Here are some design principles.

Keep it simple. Complex rituals can be difficult to understand and execute and may not resonate with your team members. Simple rituals are easy to understand and participate in and more effective in creating a sense of connection and belonging among team members.

Make it relatable. Rituals with a human touch are more effective in creating an emotional connection and response among team members. For example, if your organisation values teamwork, you might have a weekly team-building activity that is fun, interactive, and genuine.

Make it inclusive. Make sure all team members feel included and welcome to participate by accommodating different religious, cultural or personal beliefs.

Make it practical. Rituals should be practical, relevant and meaningful for the team members. Something they look forward to that positively impacts their work life. Look for rituals that help people do better in their everyday.

Make it flexible. Allow people to opt in. Be open to feedback and make adjustments as necessary. This can help ensure that the rituals meet their intended purpose and keep resonating with team members.

Make it consistent. Regularly performing rituals creates a sense of routine and predictability in the workplace, providing security and continuity. Something simple and repeated builds meaning over time.

Try stacking rituals.

Try turning ordinary routines into rituals. It's as simple as saying 'good morning' as a baseline connection. By approaching your greetings differently, you'll find they grow in meaning for you and land differently with your team.

Try stacking rituals with daily habits already in play. This aligns with BJ Fogg's approach to designing habits.[20] Fogg is a behavioural scientist who founded the Behaviour Design Lab at Stanford University. His work includes researching habits and nudging behaviour. Rituals act as nudges and are more powerful because they tap into our emotions.

Like BJ Fogg's habit design, you can design rituals using this simple formula.

```
Trigger > beginning, middle, end, > emotional reward
```

First, identify what will trigger or start the ritual. Then design the beginning, middle and end. (As with designing gatherings, pay special attention to the opening and closing.) Now, determine the emotional reward by answering the question – 'How do I want my team to feel after this ritual?'

Here's a ritual I designed when integrating a team from four newly merged entities.

We held weekly meetings for an hour. I deliberately chose a shorter, higher frequency meeting for the first year the team worked together. After the first year, we moved to two hours per fortnight which was still a higher frequency than perhaps obviously necessary. Given the significant and shared change agenda this team would need to lead in their respective businesses, I needed to rapidly build and strengthen team cohesion.

The ritual was a simple check-in at the start of our meeting. I realised I needed to connect the team on a more personal level than the self-protective interactions we started with. Hearing about people's weekends or personal lives began to break down barriers. Commonalities and contrasts became clearer and relationships deepened over time.

The *trigger* was the start of the meeting. Each person took one minute to share what was happening for them outside of work. As trust built, they started to share more about how they were feeling. We invested ten minutes at the front of each meeting to run this check-in, and it was worth it. I *began* the ritual by choosing someone at random, sharing the love between the team. After their check-in, they nominated the next person to share. We listened to each person in the group and I *ended* with my own check-in. Then I referenced some of the stories or highlights and shared something encouraging or philosophical to bring us to a close before transitioning to the agenda proper. The *emotional reward* was usually a laugh, or a virtual hug, depending on the tone of the check-ins. It worked well and many of the team cascaded the ritual into their own team meetings.

Encourage and facilitate your teams' participation in rituals by including team members in the design and encouraging them to take ownership.

Keep checking on the rituals you design. Some have a sunset clause where they gradually grow less effective as they become more familiar. Shift gears by refreshing or replacing some rituals to keep the mix fresh and engaging.

Change your rituals, change your culture.

Rituals are powerful when used on purpose and are often underestimated and undervalued in the workplace.

Remember, change your rituals, change your culture.

Experiments

Safety walks or safety interactions are rituals. Shift the impact of your next safety interaction by broadening your observations beyond the physical to include rituals. Ask about safety rituals used by the team.

Craft your own Acknowledgement of Country. Find your personal connection to culture and country and share what it means to you. Consider attending the *Acknowledge This* public training course online to build your confidence to craft and deliver your own. Research and learn about the Country on which you live and work. Many great resources are available to learn more and support you to better understand this important ritual. If you are based outside of Australia, seek to understand First Nation culture and rituals and how you can show respect.

Use music to shift the vibe in your team. Collate a team playlist and play music from it when you gather in person or online. Celebrate success with a victory dance. Play an upbeat song and get everyone up and dancing for two minutes to celebrate together. It's a quick energise and breaks up the day. It also provides plenty to bond over. I still can't unsee the GM of a regulatory team proudly and expertly doing the worm.

Shift how people see awards. Increase the value of your awards. Not the spend value but the esteem in which they are held. How valued are the awards you give out now? Consider how you can make them matter more. Make the awards ceremony more of an event, or shift from a formal to an informal approach to make the awards more accessible.

Conduct a ritual audit. Capture and list the rituals used in your team in one column. Begin with starts and finishes, beginnings and endings. Think about celebrations, commiserations and rewards. Add in how you mark occasions such as life events or cyclical business occasions. Then answer the following questions: How do they make my team feel? How do I want them to make my team feel? What do they mean today? What could they mean in the future? On a scale of 1-5, what value does the team place on each ritual? Use this audit to determine quick wins and shifts that will require a bit more effort. Engage your team in the process and conduct the audit together. Share, discuss and use the collective findings to retire and replace tired rituals, refresh ones you wish to keep or design new ones.

Tell the story behind. Uncover the story behind your organisation-wide or long-standing team rituals. Strengthen the impact of the ritual by telling your team the story. This deepens the meaning attached to the ritual, which reinforces the power of the ritual.

Reflections

How do you reward and award success? What are the success rituals in your team?

What rituals could you introduce to improve how your teams view failure? How could you ritualise failure to reinforce the importance of intelligent failure?

Which rituals have become meaningless in your team?

What daily rituals could you redesign to increase their meaning?

How do you welcome people into your team? How do you want them to feel on arrival?

How do you farewell people as they move on? What do you want them to remember?

What rituals have become habits that you may need to remember the meaning of?

8

Actions

Once upon a time, there was a US navy officer named David Marquet. He had trained extensively for a specific type of submarine, but on arrival in Pearl Harbour, he unexpectedly found himself appointed as captain of the USS Santa Fe, a different kind of nuclear-powered submarine. At the time, the Santa Fe was the worst-performing submarine in the US fleet.

As an experienced officer, Marquet was used to giving orders and taking control. He expected his crew to follow his lead. But early in his tenure, Marquet made a mistake. He unknowingly gave an impossible order, and his crew tried to follow it. This mistake became a turning point.

Marquet realised that his crew and the submarine were in danger unless he changed his leadership style. He understood that leadership should mean *giving* control rather than *taking* it and creating leaders rather than followers. He wanted to create a culture of excellence where his crew members were empowered, motivated and driven to achieve their goals.

Using his initiative, Marquet pushed for leadership at every level. He stopped giving orders and focused on giving intent. He challenged his instincts to take control and instead encouraged his crew to take ownership of their work. He made it his mission to say 'I don't know' at least once per day, role modelling vulnerability and learning by asking each crew member about their work. He implemented a rule to stop laying blame and made the crew accountable. One of his accidental mantras, 'There's no they in Santa Fe', got traction quickly. (I'm a believer in the power of rhyme and alliteration to aid memory, so I love that the rhyme helped this stick.)

At first, Marquet's crew was sceptical of his new leadership style. But within 24 hours, they started owning their mistakes and outcomes. Teamwork improved, and within 21 days, the submarine passed its first inspection from the US Admiralty.

Marquet's approach soon paid off and the Santa Fe started winning awards and promoting a highly disproportionate number of officers to submarine command. The crew's morale improved, and their performance became exceptional. Each crew member became a leader and assumed responsibility for everything they did, from clerical tasks to crucial combat decisions. They became fully engaged, contributing their total intellectual capacity every day.

The late Dr Stephen Covey spent time on the submarine with Captain Marquet and his crew. Together, they captured Marquet's shift in leadership as The Leadership Ladder. Essentially, Marquet helped his crew climb the ladder by continually levelling up their conversations.

The Leadership Ladder

Invitations		Statements
7. What have you been doing...?		7. I've been doing...
6. I've done...		6. I've done...
5. What do you intend...?		5. I intend to...
4. What would you like to do...?		4. I would like to...
3. What do you think...?		3. I think...
2. What do you see...?		2. I see...
1. I'll tell you what to do.		1. Tell me what to do?

Turn the ship around, David Marquet

Marquet's actions show the significant impact that a leader's way of leading can have on their team. He transformed a poorly performing submarine and crew into an exceptional one by giving control and creating leaders. His story is shared in his book, *Turn the ship around! A true story of turning followers into leaders.*[1]

Actions shape culture

Cultures are shaped by the actions of leaders and the actions they tolerate from others. These have a ripple effect and, sometimes, unintended consequences.

Where you spend your time and energy, what you focus on, what you say and do are all being observed by your teams. Your actions, words and attitudes are emulated by team members and shape how they think, feel and behave. Teams look to you to guide how they should respond.

The leadership challenge is, as always, to act in a way that sets the tone and models the desired behaviours. To act on purpose, with purpose. Where possible, be considered, deliberate and consistent in your actions. The opportunity is to embed this way of leading into your everyday actions through habits and ways of thinking.

Act on purpose, with purpose.

By reading this book, you've shown a willingness to lead your organisation's culture and develop your leadership.

At the core of my Cultureshift model are the two multipliers; the behaviours leaders *demonstrate* and the behaviours they *tolerate*. These actions have an outsized impact on culture.

To be clear, actions include what you say and do.

Leaders as Multipliers

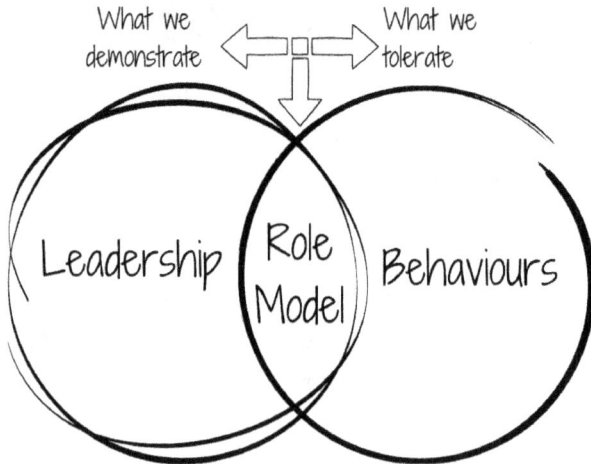

Act loudly on things that matter

In Australia, the government has recently introduced legislative changes aimed at holding organisations more accountable for sexual harassment and other forms of workplace misconduct.

One of the most significant changes is the publication of the Respect@Work report, which was commissioned following a series of high-profile cases of workplace harassment and misconduct. The report identified several areas where current workplace laws and regulations were inadequate and recommended a range of reforms to better protect workers from harassment and abuse. These changes are expected to make it much harder for organisations to sweep workplace harassment and misconduct under the carpet and to create a safer and more respectful workplace culture for all team members.

It will be interesting to see the ripple effect of the Respect@Work report in practice. I am particularly curious about how leaders respond when their organisation is in the headlines.

General Motors (GM) has made significant strides in improving its culture and leadership in recent years. Mary Barra, the CEO, has been at the forefront of these efforts, implementing various strategies and initiatives to shift the organisation's culture towards one that values accountability, transparency and inclusivity.

GM has focused on gathering feedback from team members to understand their experiences and perspectives on the company's culture. The organisation has implemented various feedback mechanisms, such as surveys and town hall meetings, to gather input from team members at all levels.

Importantly, GM has taken action to address inappropriate

behaviour and conduct not aligned with the organisation's values. In 2018, the company launched an investigation into allegations of sexual harassment and discrimination at one of its plants. The investigation resulted in the termination of several team members who were found to have engaged in inappropriate behaviour. Barra and other leaders at GM have made it clear that inappropriate behaviour and actions will not be tolerated. Barra responded to the allegations of sexual harassment by taking swift and decisive action. She publicly denounced any behaviour not in line with the company's values and committed to a zero-tolerance policy towards sexual harassment and discrimination.

In 2018, Barra announced a new program called 'Speak up for Safety', which encouraged team members to speak up about safety concerns or inappropriate behaviour. The program included training for all team members on recognising and reporting any company policy violations. Barra ordered an independent investigation into the company's handling of sexual harassment complaints, which resulted in the dismissal of several executives who had failed to take action on such complaints. She also created a new position of chief talent officer to oversee diversity and inclusion efforts and human resources.

Furthermore, Barra made it clear that GM would not settle any sexual harassment claims but would fight them in court to ensure that the company was held accountable for any wrongdoing.

Through these actions, Barra demonstrated her commitment to creating a culture of respect and inclusion at GM and her willingness to take strong measures to address any company policy violations.

GM's efforts to shift its culture and leadership have had a positive impact. In 2020, GM was named one of Forbes' best employers for diversity and recognised for its commitment to inclusion and equity.

Act now

Leaders are active, not passive.

Warren Davis, an executive at J.P. Morgan ANZ, sees leaders as those who step forward, lean in, drive change and inspire others. In a world of increasing complexity and uncertainty, we can't know everything before we act. Leaders are those who step forward into the unknown.

> # Leaders are active, not passive.

When it comes to working on your culture, don't wait for the official go-ahead. This book is full of actions you can take to shape and shift your culture.

Context and consequences

The actions and decisions leaders make ripple throughout the organisation.

By demonstrating ways of working and behaving that are culturally aligned, team members have a clear guide for expectations of their behaviour. Command and control style leadership, reinforced by a culture of strict hierarchy, enabled 'managers' to behave differently from what they expected of their 'subordinates'.

Even the language of 'subordinates' (and I include the term 'staff' here, too) indicates the kind of culture at play. Try using 'team', 'team members' or 'people' instead. I deliberately only use 'employee' when referencing a legal employment relationship. Language matters. Words are actions too.

Gaps between what you say and do have consequences. When they don't match, it impacts trust and brings doubt into the equation.

Some leaders I surveyed described culture as 'what you do when nobody is watching'.

Today team members expect transparency, authenticity and accountability from their leaders. To ask your team to do things you wouldn't do is not good leadership. It's a matter of integrity.

I love Dupont's concept of visible and felt leadership (VFL).[2] It is exactly what it says. Leaders visibly and actively lead, and team members see and feel that leadership. Leadership is demonstrated. It is active.

Picture this; your leader stands in front of a town hall-style gathering, reminding everyone to wear their safety glasses at all times when onsite. Your leader says all the right things. They are persuasive and engaging. They even support what they say with facts, statistics and examples. The whole audience recommits to wearing their safety glasses at all times. The next day you notice that even some of the more frequent offenders are wearing their safety glasses. The communication has worked.

The size of your team shapes how loudly and often you need to demonstrate. A bit like the difference in hand gestures when I'm facilitating a conversation in a board room versus the larger-than-life, more theatrical gestures necessary when I am on stage in front of a larger audience.

If you lead a team, wearing your safety glasses every day demonstrates the behaviour. You might need to remind individuals occasionally or mention it in a team meeting. You probably don't need to stand on stage doing a presentation. If you lead the site or the organisation and are visiting, consistently wearing your safety glasses will be noticed. However, just wearing your own isn't sufficient if you want to shift a culture where glasses aren't worn consistently. As an executive visiting a site, you need to wear them loudly and pull up people who are not wearing theirs.

Consistency matters too. All your good work, remembering to wear your safety glasses every day, will be undone by walking past someone who isn't wearing them and doing nothing about it. As the saying goes, the standard you walk past is the standard you accept.

> The standard you walk past is the standard you accept.

When I think about actions, I think about What, How and Why. Remember Lisa Kay's phrase, 'Leadership is relentlessly contextual'? Context is king. And culture is context. What might be acceptable in one context could be unacceptable in another. What might make you a hero in one culture could make you a villain in another. So, when we think about actions, we need to consider them in the broader context. That is, it's not just what we do; it's how we do it and why.

To really shift culture, we need to be more deliberate about our actions. We need to behave more *on* purpose and *with* purpose. That requires more conscious action and operating less in default mode. Acting on purpose means being deliberate. Acting with purpose means being conscious of why we are doing something; being clear on our intent before we act.

We also need to consider how we show up. Considering the context in which we work helps us think about the different perspectives that might be applied to our actions. Thinking about how other people might think and feel provides a more well-rounded view of our actions. By acting on purpose and with purpose, we influence how we are perceived and are congruent with what is expected of us. By being considered, deliberate and consistent in our actions, we can build trust and positively influence the culture around us.

On purpose, with purpose

As a leader, your actions set the tone for the team. Michael Henderson is a corporate anthropologist. He writes, leading is like 'chiefing'. That is, acting like the chief of a tribe. He says three things matter most when it comes to chiefing. Start the fire every day. Greet with intent. Forgive with ease.[3]

> **Start the fire every day.**

Let's consider these three actions.

What would starting the fire look like in your team? What is your team's fire? Perhaps this happens at a daily stand-up? Maybe the fire your team needs from you is fun or connection? Maybe your team needs to be reminded to look to the light on the hill – what is the goal you're chasing, or the purpose of the work you do?

Greeting with intent sounds simple, and, as we covered in Chapter Seven, it is, but it is surprisingly impactful. Just by greeting people, you can start to shift your culture. 'With intent' is important. The intention of a quick nod in passing is recognition. The intention of stopping to chat is connection. How did you greet people today? What was your intention?

And finally, forgive with ease. The first reflection point is, of course, are you forgiving? And when you forgive, is it hard work? If your team was asked, would they say you forgive with ease?

The currency of consistency

Cultures are shaped by what you pay attention to. Like any currency, attention is valuable because it is finite and scarce. People look to their leaders to signpost what matters most.

Think about this. Would you prefer your leader to be consistently unfair or inconsistently unfair? You might be surprised to learn that people prefer a consistently unfair leader because they know what to expect. Sure, we'd all prefer a consistently fair leader, but in the absence of that, most of us prefer no surprises.

> Cultures are shaped by what you pay attention to.

In a world of disruption, ambiguity and uncertainty, where we are working in the never-normal, leaders have a unique opportunity to provide a sense of predictability and continuity where they can. Regular gatherings or simple rituals can do this, as can symbols and stories. Yet the thing that is most in our control is our own behaviour; how we act. What we say and do. Being consistent or communicating clearly when there is a shift provides a sense of safety and continuity for your team.

Belinda Brosnan, C-Suite executive coach and trusted confidante partners with senior leaders to develop their unique leadership DNA. Belinda describes this as the essence and experience of leaders, as well as what they can do. She takes this one step further with DNA standing for Daily, Now, Always. Belinda's work frames the importance of consistent behaviours and consistent call-outs. 'You can put all your effort into your personal brand and aspirations, but if you don't show up congruent to that consistently, you will struggle to garner the trust and respect of your peers and team.'[4] What do you do daily, now and always? How congruent are your daily actions with what matters most? How consistent would your people say you were?

Daily, Now, Always.

Early in my career, I inherited a team in a very formal and hierarchical culture. Clearly, the previous manager's directive and restrictive style had heavily impacted the team's performance and discretionary effort. I arrived feeling like I was liberating them and met with interesting reactions when I clarified my expectations of their contribution, autonomy, collaboration and creativity.

About a third of the team was thrilled. Finally, they could work as they preferred and bubbled over with ideas for improvements they hadn't been encouraged to share. By removing the constraints, they felt free to fly and get on with things.

Another third of the team felt threatened. The safety of strict guardrails was removed and they hadn't developed the skills or confidence to act (and some days it felt like 'think') on their own. So, they stopped acting. They waited to be told what to do as if they were still caged.

The final third was so bruised by the previous regime that, even when the restraints were removed, they didn't trust it was true. They thought it was a trick or a test. Some ran away, some hid, and some stayed stuck in plain sight.

As a student of human behaviour, it was fascinating. As a young leader, it was frustrating. I'd acted the same way with everyone, but it was only working with a third of the team. The reality was that team members were bruised from their experiences, and I had to show up differently for each of them. I had to rapidly build trust with the two-thirds of the team who were stuck.

It took time, repeated messaging and consistency of actions. It took rewarding the desired behaviour and deliberately dismantling the old ways of working. It took hours of individual conversations, team discussions and repeated communication of the new expectations. It took role modelling. Always. The slightest hint of a slip was pounced upon as evidence I didn't mean it and that the shift wasn't real. Some of the team ended up self-selecting out, which was a positive outcome for them and the organisation.

After six months, the team was humming and working completely differently. It was unrecognisable from the group I met on my first day. Most of the members went on to bigger and better things. The shift was, of course, challenging, exhausting and rewarding — like most things that are worth doing.

Consistency matters. A little inconsistency matters a lot. Joseph Folkman, a behavioural statistician and author, researches trust in leadership.[5] With 360-degree assessment data from over 100,000 leaders and nearly 10,000 individual contributors, he generated a consistency index rating leaders on five items. These five criteria describe a person that is predictable and reliable.

Consistency matters.

- Is a role model and sets a good example
- Avoids saying one thing and doing another
- Honours commitments and keeps promises
- Follows through on commitments
- Willing to go above and beyond what needs to be done.

Leaders who scored in the bottom 20% overall were assessed against these five criteria. His research showed that despite some good leadership traits, their inconsistency generated an overall negative perception of their capability. Those considered inconsistent were also seen as failing to follow through, easily distracted, failing to anticipate problems until it was too late and failing to achieve agreed-upon goals. They were regarded as resisting taking steps to improve and not co-operating well with others. Their judgement was not trusted in making decisions, and their teammates did not trust them. Being inconsistent, Folkman found, led to a negative perception on almost every other competency or behaviour.

So, behaving consistently is important, but it doesn't mean being slow or resistant to change. Consistency means I know what to expect from you.

Unintended consequences

When we understand that our actions carry weight and meaning that are constantly interpreted by our teams, we also appreciate that actions have consequences. Some of which are unintended. Communication goes a long way to overcoming the assumptions which lead there.

> # Consider the consequences of your actions.

One of the fastest ways to break trust is to do something you said you wouldn't. The second is not to do something you said you would. For some, this is the definition of integrity. Both are, generally, actions within your control. Consider the consequences of your actions on your relationships, your reputation and your culture.

I once worked with the CEO of a mining organisation, who, on a site tour with the operations leaders, looked twice at a stockpile on an overflow pad. When he left an hour later, a digger and dozer were moving the material. Querying the stammering operations leaders, he realised that he had inadvertently caused the rehandle and waste by seeming to question the placement of the stockpile. The team walking with him were nervous and paid attention to everything he said and did — including what he paid attention to. Without any communication, the team assumed he was displeased and made the decision to change, resulting in thousands of dollars of rework.

Sometimes we unintentionally make matters worse. As a new leader, I learned about the Five Whys technique, which involves asking why until you get to the root cause. It's fine in theory, but *how* you ask a why question matters. Try being on the receiving end of five whys. It can get defensive. Fast. Conversations become oppositional when people are concerned about being blamed or their teammates being blamed.

There are ways to ask why so that this doesn't happen. In safety-focused industries, the adoption of 'just cultures' has helped to break down barriers to understanding what happens when things go wrong. Put simply, a just culture is the opposite of a blame culture. We ask, 'What went wrong?' instead of 'Who did that?' It's a simple shift in language with powerful results.

Anthropologists recognise that there is often a gap between what we think we do and what we actually do. IKEA employs a team of anthropologists to apply their field techniques with customers

> A simple shift in language with powerful results.

to understand customer behaviour better. A selected group of customers complete a survey and are interviewed by researchers. Following that data collection, the researchers move to observation.

In one example, customers were asked how they used the sofa in their homes. Responses included things you would expect – sitting and lying on the sofa, eating dinner in front of the television, cuddling, reading, and entertaining guests. People admitted to sitting on the arms and cushions on the back of the sofa. However, it was only through observing how families used the furniture that IKEA realised how often people sat on the floor, leaning back on their sofas. It hadn't been mentioned in the survey or interview responses.

There's a similar gap between what we *say* we do and what we *actually* do. This is a common conversation when I conduct culture diagnoses. Leaders will be adamant they conduct performance and development conversations, but team members don't share the same view. Some of this will be an execution gap (not done well), some will be a perception gap (is that what that was?), and sometimes, it will be impacted by the recency effect (how long ago was that?).

Organisational theory talks about espoused values versus values in action, or lived values. How different are the values you talk about from those you demonstrate through your actions? I was fascinated by consumer insights shared by the supermarket chain Coles. It showed the difference between the number of people who say organic fruit and vegetables are important and those who say they buy the produce. And the most interesting piece? There's an even greater gap in the data showing how many people actually bought and paid for organic vegetables.

As you reflect on your actions and behaviour, understand the difference between what you think you said or did versus what actually happened. Contrast that with how the other person received what you said or did. Feedback processes (such as 360-degree) can help with this, and you can also debrief interactions with your team and those around you. Consider the other person's perspective to understand what they might have seen or heard. Most of the time, you can't know, but being considered in your intention and the context will help tweak your approach so it will land better.

A moment that matters that's worth calling out is how you respond to things. As the Austrian psychiatrist Viktor Frankl wrote:

> *'Between stimulus and response, there is a space. In*
> *that space is our power to choose our response.'*[6]

Leadership is not just about setting direction and making decisions; it's also about setting an example for others to follow. Your actions, words and attitudes significantly impact the people around you, especially your team members. As a leader, you need to understand that you are role-modelling all the time. People are watching. The question is, what are you role modelling?

When leaders model the behaviour they expect from others, it sends a powerful message that they are committed to the same standards and values that they expect from their team.

A leader's attitude is contagious and can profoundly impact the state of their team. Your optimism and enthusiasm create a positive and productive environment, which helps boost the morale and motivation of your team. In contrast, feeling negative and pessimistic can contribute to a toxic atmosphere, demotivating and discouraging those around you. In

A leader's attitude is contagious.

that state, you're focusing inward and probably not noticing what is happening around you.

In positive and productive cultures, leaders listen and are open and approachable. They are easy to talk to and more likely to build trust and respect with their team. When team members feel comfortable approaching their leader, they share their ideas, concerns and feedback, providing opportunities for improvement. Listening enables you to understand others' perspectives and make decisions that benefit the entire team.

Alan Lowthorpe has led many digital led transformations.[7] His view is that culture is what people *don't* do or observe without commenting, as much as it's about what they do, think and say. When poor behaviour or counter-cultural comments are allowed, this sends implicit signals that the behaviour is acceptable — even if it is counter to the stated or aspirational culture of the organisation.

In our conversation, Alan shared a few examples. When leaders have corridor conversations that impact, or should include, the broader team, it can undermine the credibility of official communications. Team members then question if leaders are truly saying what they think or if there is a parallel agenda.

Alan recognises the power of greetings and acknowledgement when leaders walk around the office. When leaders don't acknowledge or greet team members, it reinforces the distance between them. It discourages team members from approaching their leaders with both ideas and issues. He also cautions leaders who show little interest in their teams and focus on their own worlds. 'It leads to team members feeling like commodities in service of the leader.' Alan believes the role of the leader is to enable and empower team members to do their magic.

Leaders who tolerate negative behaviour or lack of accountability, risk creating a culture of complacency and low performance.

In a recent conversation, Antony Moore, from the Lottery Corporation, said that leaders who do not hold people to account, undermine culture. Team members see these behaviours being accepted, which becomes how we do things around here. That renders any attempt at driving the culture in accordance with vision and principles almost useless as they simply become words on a page. He thinks great leaders call poor behaviours to account in a respectful manner, demonstrating support for the culture and the vast majority of people in the organisation that embrace it. In a great culture, it isn't just leaders acting this way; it's everybody.

Leaders must be willing to hold themselves and others accountable for their actions and take action to address inappropriate behaviour or misaligned actions.

Take the oar

One of my favourite tools to share with leaders and organisations when shifting culture is OARBED. Every day, we choose between taking the OAR (Ownership, Accountability, Responsibility) or staying in BED (Blame, Excuses, Denial).

Christopher Avery, the creator of the OARBED model, has written several books that discuss the framework and its applications, including *Teamwork Is An Individual Skill*.[8] His books provide guidance on how to use the OARBED model to improve personal and team performance and build a culture of accountability and ownership.

An OARsome culture (sorry, hard to resist) is full of people who take ownership of their actions, are accountable for the results of those actions, and take responsibility for their impact on others and the organisation. Yet OARful cultures (sorry, had to be done) are rife with BED (Blame, Excuses, Denial). People tend to blame others for their mistakes, make excuses for their failures, and deny responsibility for their actions. Teams are BEDridden (sorry, couldn't help it). Of course, this is a simplistic view. No organisation has all of its people operating at 100% OAR or 100% BED. The reality is that OARBED is a continuum.

The OARBED model introduces language for your team to call out behaviour that is either OAR or BED. I love watching this concept catch on and filter through an organisation. Watching how teams take this and make it their own is fascinating. It highlights the choices we make each day – to take the oar or to stay in bed.

Where are your actions on the OARBED continuum? Where are people in your team on the continuum? How can you use this as a call to action for you and your team?

Words matter

One of the most powerful and pervasive everyday shifts we can make is to change our language. Introducing and using specific words or phrases reinforces what's important. Organisation or even team-specific words contribute to a feeling of belonging. Shared language can be a powerful unifier. Playing with words and phrases can harness the power of memes that make your key messages catchy and repeatable. You'll improve the half-life of the message by increasing the stickiness of the words you use.

> Shared language can be a powerful unifier.

Like all strengths, if you overplay this, it becomes a weakness. Some cultures become jargon bound, which increases the entry barrier for new people. Words then become exclusive — and not in a good way. When people feel excluded, language creates divides. While this is often unintentional, using jargon can creep up on you. Mechanisms to combat this, such as wikis or dictionaries, can be included in onboarding. Checking for understanding is one of those leader actions that is easy to do, and easy not to do.

As leaders, we need to be accountable for our actions and hold others accountable for theirs. Lead by example and hold yourself to the same standards and expectations that you have for your team members. Doing so ensures that everyone is working towards the same goals and standards and improves the likelihood that team members will take responsibility for their actions and their impact on the team and organisation. Encourage regular check-ins, provide feedback, and track progress to help your team meet their goals. It's a matter of balancing support and guidance.

Take action

Consider acting on purpose to tackle a significant cultural issue in your organisation. Email and Messenger traffic has exploded, and the more people you lead, the heavier the weight of your inbox. You can take action to shift the email culture in your teams.

As with meetings, there are plenty of resources on how to do email better. If you're up for the challenge, I recommend Dermot Crowley's book *Smart Work*[9] and Cal Newport's *Digital Minimalism*[10] and *Deep Work.*[11]

Whatever improvements you identify, harness your culture instead of taking a policy approach. Lead by example. Incite an email revolution. Spark a movement. Continue accepting a culture that allows BCC and group emails to substitute for communication or advocate for real connection and move off email. Watch out for slacktivism (nobody wants a slacktivist — an armchair activist), which is full of opinions and few solutions. Solutions only solve problems when they are implemented, so push for action.

'Never underestimate the power of a small
group of committed people to change the world.
In fact, it is the only thing that ever has.'
— Margaret Mead[12]

Shifting requires staying power

Remember, a chosen culture cannot be created overnight; it requires consistent and persistent efforts to develop and maintain, and your everyday actions play a crucial role. By consistently role-modelling the behaviour you expect from your team and fostering a culture of accountability and responsibility, you can create a positive and productive environment that supports the success of your organisation.

Culture is caught, not taught.

Culture is ongoing, not a one-time task or action. While shifting culture requires active leadership, sustaining existing culture also takes action. It will gradually devolve unless you act to protect and nurture it.

Remember, culture is caught, not taught.

Experiments

Conduct an attention audit. Over the past week, what has your leader, or a peer, paid attention to that influenced your actions? What have you paid attention to that your team will have noticed? What is something important that you have not paid attention to that might need putting back on your radar and that of your team?

Promote learning from mistakes. Share a story about a big mistake you made. What happened and what did you learn from it? Be vulnerable and show that everyone makes mistakes; we are all works in progress.

Start a movement. Pick something that is a pain point (such as my email challenge) and start talking about how it could be different. Introduce an alternative option. Call out the consequences of the current actions. Garner allies and share widely. Inspire action. Start a movement.

Play with memes. What messages could you turn into memes? Who are the wordsmiths in your team or organisation that could assist you? Identify an important message and practise developing memes or catch cries to make it stickier. Consider the best modes or methods of communication to share the memes you develop.

Go back to basics. We all know the basics of leadership. For a refresher, check out Google's Project Aristotle for a useful list.[13] Assess your typical day and week. What basics of leader actions have you let slide? What reminders could you implement to keep this front of mind? What else could you do to bring back everyday leader actions?

Reflections

Have I done what I said I would do? Have I said what I would do?

What are my responsibilities here? Where can I take ownership and accountability?

How can I accept what's happening without blaming someone else?

How did I contribute to this?

What could I be doing differently? How can I make a difference?

How could I start the fire every day? Am I greeting with intent? Do I forgive with ease?

How can I find a win/win?

What behaviours did I role model today? What did I role model in tricky or important interactions?

Who does this well? What can I adopt or adapt from them?

9

Symbols

If we only think of symbols in terms of Da Vinci Code-style cryptology, we'll miss many of the signs that surround us in our culture every day.

In 2022, my husband walked the Camino Francés, some 900 kilometres through coastal and regional Spain from the French border to Santiago de Compostela. Pilgrims, referred to as pellegrino, have been walking camino trails for more than 1000 years. After I waved goodbye at the traditional starting point of Puente de Santiago (Santiago Bridge) in Irún, his first day involved walking 27 kilometres through several small towns, heading to San Sebastian. Google Maps indicated this would take roughly four hours. It took him nearly twice that.

Those walking a camino follow symbols to find their way. These aren't like road signs. While there are official signs at every cathedral in Europe, on the St James Way, pilgrims follow little yellow arrows indicating the way, often painted on fences, roads, gutters and trees. They can be easy to miss.

On his first day, he missed one, resulting in more hours of walking than he had planned. Within a few days, however, he had trained his eyes to spot the yellow arrows showing the way. On arrival in Santiago de Compostela 30 days later, he and his fellow travellers told many stories about the little yellow arrows. Each one sighted brought a sense of satisfaction and came to mean they were closer to achieving their goal.

Another symbol of the camino is the scallop shell. Pilgrims hang scallop shells from their backpacks to symbolise the journey they are on. There are many different camino paths and the scallop lines uniting at the base of the shell symbolise the many paths to Santiago de Compostela. Alongside the yellow arrows marking the way are images of scallop shells. You can see symbols of scallops on walls, cobblestones, signposts and churches.

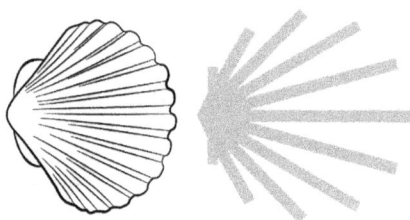

Symbols from El Camino.

In his book, *Sand Talk: How indigenous thinking can save the world*, Tyson Yunkaporta explains how lines, symbols and shapes help us learn, remember and make sense of the world.[1] Since cave drawings and early alphabets such as Egyptian hieroglyphs, humans have used symbols to convey meaning. Discovering and interpreting artefacts are a way to understand a culture.

> Defn: artefact(s) /ˈɑːtɪfakt/
> an object made by a human being,
> typically one of cultural or historical
> interest.

Symbols are a visual shorthand for team members. They represent things and, as such, are open to interpretation. Symbols can be anything that conveys meaning from words on a page, images, flags, trophies, workplace design, logos or the colours of positions on organisational charts. It can also include the allocation of perks, such as the car park nearest the lift or the office with the best view. Symbols have the power to speak the unspoken and engage our emotions. Every culture is rich with symbols.

Once you see them, it's hard to unsee.

Clues to your culture

Symbols play a crucial role in shaping workplace culture, serving as a powerful tool for reinforcing and communicating what matters and the expectations of an organisation. Symbols are breadcrumbs to help you see your culture at work. They communicate values, beliefs and expectations and can serve as a constant reminder of the organisation's purpose and priorities.

> Symbols are breadcrumbs to help you see your culture.

Symbols set the tone — particularly in times of uncertainty when people look for clues. In the absence of communication, they will latch on to symbols and what they might mean. The marketing director not holding the lift doors open for the CFO could be made to mean many things, depending on your filters and perspectives. The CEO building a bigger office with a personal bathroom and kitchen sends a message.

The reality is that each organisation's culture has many symbols, often layers upon layers, and each of these is interpreted in as many ways as there are team members. Our brains register symbols subconsciously, constantly assessing our environment.

You are most acutely aware of symbols when you first join an organisation or team. You are looking for clues. Your eyes are fresh, noticing things you won't even be aware of in a few months. Those symbols become part of the furniture and blend into the background. You also have a heightened awareness of symbols in your surroundings whenever you feel under threat, in times of change or uncertainty or if you are anxious about something. In these circumstances, your brain is looking for signals of threat or safety and may bring symbols to your awareness to assess meaning.

Our brains are wired to perceive mixed messages as threats. Consider this example that you may recognise. An IT team moved away from dedicated, individual support to a help desk operating model. Communications with team members shared the rationale for moving and a commitment to maintaining service levels.

As part of the change, the technology support team moved to be co-located rather than embedded on different floors with their clients. Their new floor had the added advantage of higher security, which was considered a positive outcome. However, other teams could not access the new floor, so no one could visit to seek assistance. All replies from the help desk were now anonymous, and access to support was via email only. Connection and relationships were cut, and clients no longer knew who they were dealing with. Understanding the client context was lost, and the NPS for the team plummeted.

In this instance, efficiency came at the cost of effectiveness, and many of us have experienced it in large organisations. The aggregation of service functions makes sense, but the way the shift was handled meant clients experienced mixed messages. Verbal and written communication said service would remain the same, yet symbolically, the doors were locked and names were removed from emails. Yes, this shift could have been managed better, and perhaps a phased transition from high touch to standardised service would have improved outcomes. But one of the main reasons this shift was very bumpy was the distrust and suspicion caused by mixed messages.

Symbols communicate the organisation's purpose and values to customers, the community and other stakeholders, although we aren't always aware of the symbols at play, internally or externally. Symbols communicate expectations for behaviour and performance. For example, a dress code policy can signal the level of professionalism and formality expected in the workplace. A remote-first, work-from-anywhere policy can indicate trust and autonomy. These policies are unlikely to have those messages as a stated objective, but that's the message they send and what is received or perceived by team members.

Symbols add colour to your culture.

Symbols add colour to your culture. One of the most common examples is an organisation's logo or brand, which can serve as a rallying point for team members, creating a sense of unity and shared identity. It is a constant reminder of the organisation's purpose and priorities.

Symbols at work

Like rituals, symbols are often underestimated aspects of workplace culture. Their impact can be easily overlooked because they are often subtle, unseen or not always overtly acknowledged.

Aurecon, a design, engineering and advisory company, was one of Australia's first employers to introduce visual employment contracts.[2] The company's purpose is to bring ideas to life, to imagine and co-create a better future for people and the planet with their clients. A cross-functional team, drawn from people and culture, legal, communication and graphic designers, reimagined the employment contract using visual communication. It ended up looking like a comic strip.

More than 5000 words were eliminated to create a succinct, user-friendly, easily understood employment contract. It's an unconventional approach with trust at its core and sets the tone for the employment relationship between team members and the organisation. Aurecon's development approach mirrored how it works with clients, so the process was familiar to team members. How the contract was developed was as symbolic as the end outcome.

Another great use of symbols is how their Aurecon Attributes are celebrated. These describe their 'way of being' and are a collection of qualities that 'make us who we are'. On Aurecon's careers page, you can take a short quiz to assess which attributes are strongest in you.[3] They range from inquisitive and co-creative to unconventional and fearless. Aurecon acknowledges that no individual is expected to have every attribute, but they build teams that collectively have them all. Onboarding includes a coloured coffee cup with your strongest attribute, and a quick glance around a meeting shows the combination of attributes in the room. It highlights individual contribution and collective strength. It's a clever use of symbols reinforcing what matters at Aurecon.

Workplace design

The physical environment in workplaces is usually symbol rich. The layout, decor and overall design of a workspace can communicate a lot about the organisation's culture. An open office layout with plenty of natural light and plants can signal a focus on collaboration and innovation, while a more traditional, hierarchical arrangement can indicate a more formal and traditional culture.

Prominent safety walkways painted bright yellow through a distribution centre and prevalent signage are a clear sign that safety is important. A big four consulting or legal firm's upper floor offices in a modern tower on the harbour or river, with plush reception and meeting rooms, send messages about status and success. The full-height atrium in the centre of Coles Support Centre at Tooronga hosts a vibrant food court with MasterChef talent cooking for team members and giant screens promoting community and customer images across multiple levels. Symbols of connection and collaboration with teams across levels place customers and the community at the centre.

Jacob Morgan, author and work futurist, describes three elements of employee experience in his book, *The Employee Experience Advantage.*[4] These are culture, technology and place. He describes *place* as the physical or built space where employees work, including what they see, touch, hear and smell.

Melissa Marsden is a workplace dynamics strategist who has designed workplaces for more than 20 years. With the shift to remote and hybrid working, work 'place' has been a hot topic, and many organisations are rethinking how they use space. Mel's book, *The Next Workplace* responds to the question, 'What does our workplace look like when we no longer need to "go" to work?'.[5] Mel shares how zoning elevates the floor plan to shape behaviour by deliberately using space and flow. She gives examples of clients walking candidates through workspaces (designed to reflect the organisation's culture) to see their reaction.

Actions are symbols too

Actions are symbols too. While anthropologists would say symbols are generally things or physical artefacts, we cannot forget how symbolic actions can be. Princess Diana's televised hug of a patient with AIDS in the 1980s is an example of a symbolic action that confronted the fears and impacted the perspectives of millions of people around the globe.

Actions are symbols too.

While few people envision having that kind of ripple effect, we need to recognise that our actions convey meaning. Cutting someone off while they are talking has meaning. Ignoring someone as you walk past them will be attributed meaning. Arriving late to meetings is given meaning. People look to leaders' actions as an indication of what is important, how they should feel about something and as a gauge of what kind of person they are. Applying meaning to a simple action shifts it to a ritual or a symbol. It can be daunting to reflect on the symbolism of your everyday, inadvertent actions. It can also be empowering to realise that you have the opportunity to shift people's perspectives through your actions or leading by example.

Chairs, car parks and fridges

Having collected countless examples of cultural symbols over the years, the highest frequency of negative symbols goes to car parks, where someone sits and how food in the fridge is managed.

These perks are all symbols of a pecking order. For example, a prime parking spot may be seen as a perk reserved for senior leaders or high-performing team members, while a less desirable parking spot may indicate lower status or a less important role. Similarly, a corner office with a view may be seen as a symbol of power and prestige, compared with a smaller or less desirable office. These symbols can create a sense of hierarchy within the workplace and may lead to feelings of resentment or unfairness among team members.

> **Perks are all symbols of a pecking order.**

I have fond memories of one general manager's response to feedback about 'his' car park. He was adamant he did not have an assigned park. He'd deliberately removed all signs allocating parks upon starting his role and felt strongly about not having special treatment. From his perspective, he just parked in the closest available park each day. 'Yes', the team chirped in response, 'your car park'. The GM had failed to appreciate that the rest of the team left that space free because it was deemed his.

We were discussing and myth-busting the unwritten rules of culture at his site. It got even better when he declared the same thing about his seat at the boardroom table. 'I just sit at the closest empty seat to the door when I come in.' Of course, this was the seat the team left for him as his designated seat. The GM was genuinely confounded.

Myth-busting the unwritten rules of culture.

He had no idea. Luckily, the team's sense of humour helped them navigate through these realisations, and the GM then delighted in parking and sitting in different spots each day.

Stories told about car parks range widely. In one organisation, it was said that someone had to die before you could be allocated a space. The long-tenured people soaked up all the available parks and the waiting list was long and prioritised based on tenure rather than need. In another organisation, a sales leader shared that his negotiations were hampered when a major customer passed two Ferraris, owned by the CEO and CFO, parked in prime position by the front door to the office. The customer was convinced the organisation was making too much money, and negotiations became quite heated.

With the shift to hybrid work, we might think that car parks have dropped down the list. However, with a reduced footprint and dropping demand, many organisations have reduced the number of parks available, leading to even more stories of warped allocations, ongoing grumbles and poor choices.

It's important for organisations to consider the potential impact of these symbols on culture and ensure that the allocation of such resources is fair and transparent. One way around this is to use alternative ways of allocation, such as rotation or a lottery system. This allows equal opportunities and can reduce resentment among the team members. With more hybrid working arrangements in place, parking allocations present a chance to disrupt the way things have always been done.

I've included fridges as a bit of fun, but the fridge can be a workplace battleground. Google images of workplace fridge rules, and you'll see milk clubs and fridge padlocks as a start. Let's contrast a few workplace fridges and see what kind of culture they represent.

As a manager in financial services, I inherited the drinks fridge under my desk with an implied responsibility to monitor day drinking. The unwritten rules were that having a drink after 5pm on a weekday and after 4pm on Friday was ok. Compare that with a government agency where milk, tea and coffee were not supplied, and participants in the workshop I was facilitating kindly offered to gift me a teabag and a teaspoon of sugar at the morning break.

It's a very different experience to facilitating at Coca-Cola Amatil's offices, where post-mix soft drink is available on tap. Different again, is working on mine sites where the nearest lunch outlet is more than a 20-minute drive away, so everyone brings a packed lunch (and the stacking of containers by a bunch of engineers appears to defy gravity). And last but not least, the boutique drinks available in the fridge in the top legal firm's client meeting rooms compared with what the team have access to behind the public areas.

It is tempting to discount the symbolism associated with a fridge and focus on more serious symbols. It's hard for a team member to buy the focus on high-trust messaging from the CEO and the efforts of leaders and the HR team to simplify policies and encourage greater autonomy and collaboration when someone is stealing your lunch every day.

Likewise, it's difficult to have confidence in a focus on gender balance in construction when no maternity uniforms are available, female toilets are only in one spot on site, and women are penalised for needing longer breaks to get to and from the facilities.

Hidden Figures, a movie set at NASA in the 1960s, highlighted how much equal access to bathroom facilities matters.[6] Yet there are many worksites in male-dominated industries in Australia today where women face the same challenges. Announcing targets for women in leadership and 50/50 recruitment for roles matters little when the basics don't tell the same story.

When I am working with an organisation, I look for signs that provide clues to the culture. Sometimes they are positively framed, such as, 'Please keep the door closed'. Signs are powerful behaviour nudges, for example, 'Remember to wear your safety glasses' or, 'Have you left a clean desk?'

I look for the number of signs telling people what to do, where they are located and, importantly, what messages they send. Rule-bound organisations and controlling cultures often display more signs than others. These are not colourful posters promoting events such as Steptember, or health reminders in strategic places. Rather, these signs typically include the word 'don't'.

Signs and posters help communicate what matters in your culture.

We notice when things stand out.

Ignore the little things at your own risk. Many culture change programs have been slowed or reversed by everyday workplace behaviour and symbols.

It's a matter of congruence. We notice when things stand out.

Symbols can be like paint on the walls; it's there all around us, all the time. It shapes the way we see our organisation. We may not notice if all the walls are cracked and peeling, but once we paint one wall, the issues elsewhere become more obvious.

Similarly, you can't just update one symbol. It will stand out for all the wrong reasons. Instead, tackle a constellation of symbols, starting with those that matter most, are most visible or provide the quickest wins.

> # You can't just update one symbol.

First impressions

Before joining an organisation and in their first 90 days, prospective and new team members are acutely aware of symbols and their possible meaning. They are looking for clues about what to expect and what might be expected of them. They are looking for unsaid or unwritten meaning — to feel safe.

When I speak with leaders about their onboarding experience, they start with swag.

> Defn. Swag refers to the welcome kit full of merch. and goodies sent to new starters on arrival in new workplace.

Swag can be deeply symbolic and impactful or cheap and cheerful landfill. Sustainability matters to candidates and team members, with one in four job candidates saying the environmental record of organisations is a major factor when accepting a role.[7]

Michelle Williams, chief people officer for The Lottery Corporation, and her team have led the shift to tailored onboarding gifts, with the added benefit of avoiding unwanted drink bottles and mousepads ending up in landfill. New starters are sent a link to a site where they can choose from a range of branded shirts in a range of colours and sizes, along with a selection of small, branded gifts of their choice.

One of The Lottery Corporation's principles is creating joyful moments, which plays out across its brand and culture. Of course, the merchandise is only part of their onboarding experience. Throughout the organisation, symbols of joyful moments are seen on the walls and in the halls. Team members are welcomed in the same way. Like The Lottery Corporation, progressive organisations are moving beyond swag to a more personalised and meaningful onboarding experience.

Pride might seem a little old school, but genuine pride in the workplace can significantly impact team member engagement, motivation and overall performance. Onboarding is a necessary time to connect team members with the purpose and expectations of their new organisation and instil a sense of pride.

Leaders can foster pride in the workplace by utilising symbols to communicate the organisation's purpose, priorities and sense of identity. Logos and brands can be a rallying point for team members, creating a sense of unity and shared identity. When team members feel a sense of pride and connection to the organisation, they are more likely to be engaged and motivated to contribute to its success.

The physical environment can also foster pride in the workplace. A well-designed, attractive and functional workspace can create a sense of pride and ownership among team members. Elements like artwork, plants and natural light create a sense of warmth and positivity in the workplace, contributing to a sense of pride and connection. A well-maintained workspace can also be a result of pride. Housekeeping, or the lack of it, is always on a safety walk checklist. Poor housekeeping is often a sign of poor engagement. Fostering pride in the workplace is not just about symbols but rather about creating an environment where team members feel valued, respected and included.

Leaders as symbols

As leaders, we must be conscious of the symbols we are communicating, whether they are intentional or not. Many leaders I've coached say they have an open-door policy. They tell their teams that they have an open-door policy. Yet these leaders often work in offices while their teams work in an open-plan environment. And these same leaders close their doors while on the phone, doing quiet work or in meetings.

When I ask them to track how many hours in the day their doors are physically open, they are often quite shocked. I also ask them to track how often someone comes to their door each day without an appointment. Clearly, sometimes I'll be coaching some leaders on delegation and reducing the number of visitors, but generally the conversation shifts to the symbolism of the closed door versus the spoken words, 'My door is always open'. These leaders are genuinely shocked when they reflect on this simple symbol. Yet each of us sends many inadvertent messages each week.

It has always sat rather uncomfortably with me, but it certainly holds true that our clothing symbolises our identity. I'm delighted to see a general shift in workplaces and society to more relaxed expectations of dress at work. Uniforms and branded gear remain in many industries – both frontline service roles and operational roles. Unofficial uniforms are tied to belonging but can also be a clue to a 'fitting in' culture, as described by Brené Brown.

> *'Fitting in is the opposite of belonging. We feel a sense of belonging when we can show up as our true selves, bring our talents and our perspectives, and be seen, and know that we matter, and that we're a part of something.'* [8]

> # Symbols offer clues, so be a detective.

Symbols offer clues, so be a detective. Seek out and understand the symbols at play in your culture. What meaning do they hold for your team members? By understanding the power of symbols, you can harness them to release you from your legacy culture and shift toward your chosen culture.

Change symbols to shift your culture

Symbols can be a powerful tool for leaders to shift culture. By using the power of visual cues and messaging, leaders can create a sense of unity and shared identity among team members and communicate new values and expectations. These symbols can serve as a constant reminder of the organisation's purpose and what matters most. However, they alone are not enough; leaders must lead by example and be transparent and consistent in their efforts to shift culture.

Boeing, one of the largest aerospace companies in the world, has experienced significant cultural challenges in recent years. The company, known for its iconic planes like the 747 and 787, faced intense scrutiny following two deadly crashes involving its 737 MAX aircraft. These incidents led to investigations and revelations of cultural problems within the company.

One of the main issues with Boeing's culture was a focus on profit and production over safety and quality. This was evidenced by decisions to cut corners and rush the development of the 737 MAX, resulting in critical flaws that led to the two crashes. The company's leaders were also criticised for their lack of transparency and accountability in addressing the issues.

To address these cultural challenges, Boeing implemented a series of changes to its leadership, rituals, symbols and stories. The company hired new executives, including the role of chief safety officer, as a symbol of the importance of prioritising safety and quality in all aspects of the business. Boeing created a new product and services safety function to oversee and improve safety across the organisation. The company changed rituals and symbols to reinforce its focus on safety and quality. For example, they introduced new training programs and checklists to ensure all team members knew the procedures and protocols.

In addition to shifting symbols, Boeing held gatherings, such as town halls and team member forums, to promote open communication and transparency. These events allowed team members to share their concerns and ideas for improving the company's culture.

Boeing leaders shared stories of the importance of safety and quality, emphasising these values as the core of the company's mission. These stories have been shared through internal communications, training programs and other organisation-wide initiatives.

One notable example of symbolic leadership action at Boeing was the decision by CEO Dennis Muilenburg to forgo his 2019 bonus in light of the 737 MAX crisis. His action demonstrated a commitment to accountability and a willingness to take responsibility for the organisation's mistakes.

While there is still work to do, these changes have demonstrated Boeing is prepared to prioritise safety and quality over profit and production. The company has made progress in shifting its culture and rebuilding trust with its stakeholders.

One common way organisations use symbols to shift culture is to create a new logo or brand that represents the organisation's new direction and focus. This can serve as a rallying point for team members and be used in marketing materials, uniforms, and other branding efforts to communicate the new culture to customers, the community and other stakeholders. The trick, of course, is having previously distributed all your team merchandise and swag....

Culture clash

Mergers are often moments of truth for cultures. They can be risky due to potential clashes. The ability to merge organisational cultures often determines whether a merger's value is realised.

Culture clashes can lead to communication breakdowns, misunderstandings and employee turnover. It's crucial to consider cultural fit, or compatibility, during deal evaluation and due diligence. The failure of the DaimlerChrysler merger highlights the importance of this. Decision-making at Daimler was methodical, while Chrysler's was creative and unstructured. Daimler's salaries were conservative, but much less so at Chrysler. Both companies were organised differently. The result was a failed merger that cost Daimler around USD60 billion. Other recent international examples include Kraft Heinz and the T-Mobile-Sprint mergers.

> **Mergers are often moments of truth for cultures.**

PwC's 2019 *Creating Value Beyond the Deal* reported on value creation from mergers and acquisitions (M&A) from 2016-2019.[9] It found that 82% of companies that said significant value was destroyed in their latest acquisition lost more than 10% of key team members following the transaction. Cultural issues impacted value in 65% of M&A.

Unfortunately, culture gets little attention; only half of the executives surveyed said it was a key element of their integration programs. Results ranging from culture clash to culture congruence and culture compatibility refer to the degree to which the cultures of merging companies can live together. It's a critical factor in the success of mergers and acquisitions.

Yet for most transactions, decisions are made on the deal, and post-transaction teams plan for cultural barriers. Organisations typically conduct cultural assessments and appoint cultural integration teams to manage cultural differences proactively.

Put culture at the heart of the deal.

One of PwC's three main recommendations is to put culture at the heart of the deal. Naturally, I agree.

The initial evaluation should consider cultural compatibility and assess it during due diligence. When leading my first major culture integration post-acquisition, I realised how little data and intel had been gathered during due diligence. From then on, I agitated to include more than people demographics and executive talent in both evaluation and due diligence activities. I built internal playbooks for the due diligence teams.

Knowing more means you can do better. Symbols matter, but a genuine focus on value creation and culture has a greater (symbolic) impact than changing the logo. According to PwC, 30% of organisations say they prioritised rebranding on Day One, which all but 2% later admitted should not have been a priority.[10]

Instead, focus on what matters most. Include funding for people integration and culture development in the initial valuation and budget. Focusing on and investing in the integration experience for leaders and team members will increase the likelihood of, and accelerate, getting to value, faster. Investing in the coming together, determining what is shared and what is not, connecting people and integrating systems will contribute to the success of the new organisation. With the uncertainty, unknowns and unknowables inherent in mergers and acquisitions, it is the relationships and willingness of your people to go beyond that will make or break the success of the merger. Culture gives you the capacity and readiness to respond when things don't go according to plan. Ignore this investment at your own risk.

Protect the intangibles

When multinational company Unilever acquired ice cream makers Ben & Jerry's, their challenge was to lift Ben & Jerry's commerciality and fiscal discipline while protecting the valuable intangibles of their goodwill and unique culture. Corporate social responsibility (CSR), creativity and fun are cornerstones of Ben & Jerry's culture. When it comes to symbols, these play a good game.

When Unilever appointed veteran French executive Yves Couette as the CEO of Ben & Jerry's, he was greeted by an Eiffel Tower made from ice cream tubs, Edith Piaf songs, and team members wearing berets and dark glasses. The new CEO used strong symbolism from the outset, arriving in casual clothes and mucking in alongside team members. Couette reinforced the importance of 'doing good' by addressing the concerns of customers and team members about the continued commitment to CSR. In a unique, culturally aligned way to develop commercial capability from the leadership team to the frontline, a new financial acumen course based on a lemonade stand was developed and rolled out.[11] It's a great example of delivering what's required in a culturally aligned way.

Refreshing the space

Symbolically, your places of work may need a refresh. I'm not recommending a ritual cleansing of your office space with a smudging ceremony, but there is some merit to removing the ghosts and lingering remains of the past culture that may be haunting your workplace, attached to cultural artefacts or embodied in colours, logos and other symbols.

Changing the physical environment is a powerful symbol when shifting culture.

When Suncorp and Promina, two large, equal-sized financial services organisations, merged, the property footprint was realigned with newly formed teams drawn from both businesses moving together into new locations. Much thought went into workplace design, forming collaboration villages across three floors that came together in a central kitchen and dining zone on the middle floor. The overarching Suncorp Group branding was also refreshed, and a new purpose statement was created for the new combined organisation.

By redesigning the office layout, decor and overall design, leaders can communicate a new focus on collaboration, innovation, or other values. This can be done by creating open workspaces, incorporating natural light and plants, or using bold and bright colours to signal a shift towards a more dynamic and creative culture. Some workplace design incorporates scent learning from premium retail and hotel experience design. Will we see the rise of signature workplace scents?

P.S. Spring cleans are not just for the physical environment. Review your technology landscape for legacy symbols too. Intranets are notorious for harbouring old content.

Respect the past

To shift your culture, you need to refresh or replace the symbols in your organisation. Once you've identified your existing images, assess whether they need to be refreshed or replaced. Also, consider what else you could introduce to reinforce the shift to your chosen culture.

Replacing a symbol is simple; however, like most people-related actions, it's all about *how* you do it. Respect for the past or prevailing culture is important. Disposing of symbols carelessly or disrespecting them can backfire and result in resistance to your chosen culture. An effective way to remove them is to use a ritual.

Continental Airlines successfully changed its culture to be less bureaucratic and more team-oriented. Leaders used a ritual burning of their heavy 800-page policy manual in the car park to signal they were serious about busting bureaucracy. The new manual was only 80 pages. This action symbolised forthcoming cultural changes and provided a highly shareable story for team members. Additionally, they redecorated office spaces and repainted their fleet of planes, again symbolising the new way of doing things.[12] In both this and the Suncorp examples, old symbols were visibly replaced with new ones that aligned with the chosen shifts.

Change the story

Refreshing a symbol is useful when it is well-known, and your team is attached and engaged. The process can involve rebranding or repositioning. It sometimes consists of telling the story surrounding the symbol in a way that aligns more with the chosen culture than the prevailing one. Alternatively, you could move the symbol from something current to one that belongs in your historical context. For example, 1970s photos highlighting colourful choices of workwear that may not exactly be safe or appropriate today can move to a collection of historical images rather than pride of place. What could be showcased instead? What symbolises the messages you want to send today?

When Suncorp and Promina merged in 2007, it was one of Australia's largest corporate mergers. I led the integration of people and culture for the commercial and personal insurance divisions, later becoming the first head of culture for the merged organisation.

Initial planning focused on combining the best of both (BOB) into a newly formed culture. This approach worked for the banking, wealth and corporate teams. However, there were more than 25 personal insurance brands within the businesses, each with a unique culture. BOB wasn't going to work, so we worked to best of all (BOA).

With insurance as the bulk of the combined businesses, delivering a successful merging of leadership and culture was vital. In addition to the widespread updating of symbols, we utilised rituals to support the integration of teams. Before any structural changes, leaders and teams from different organisations came together to share perspectives and approaches. All teams doing integration work were visibly balanced, with representatives from both merged entities. Communication messages were co-branded initially and then transitioned to the brand of the merged organisation.

The symbol my integration program team chose to represent us was coloured socks. Yes, coloured socks. The idea was that while we might be wearing the new uniform of the merged business and appear fully integrated, people would still be attached to their heritage brand during the two-year integration period; the AAMI team still wore red socks, the Shannons team wore black and white checked socks and the GIO team wore blue socks. Socks became the symbol of allegiance. We saw them as something that might not be immediately obvious, but you might catch a glimpse or someone might show you. The internal branding on all our project documents was an array of coloured socks pegged on a clothesline. This served as a reminder to acknowledge and honour the heritage of different teams and actively work to shift allegiance to the newly forming organisation.

In meetings, our project team would declare they were wearing their coloured socks to deliberately represent and contribute the perspective of someone from that brand. While developed for internal use, it resonated outside our team too. I was fascinated to see the emergence of the phrase, 'What colour socks are they wearing?' when questioning where someone might have been coming from, or 'I've got my red socks on' to acknowledge and call out their personal bias when it came to a discussion point.

Of course, the technology team had to take it one step further and quickly introduced the concept of 'hidden' allegiance by talking about what colour underwear someone was wearing. It was a shorthand way of identifying someone who wasn't declaring their allegiance.

When we shifted to new structures and brought the top 100 leaders together to focus forward, the CEO stood on stage and pulled up his trousers to flash his green socks. It was a symbol that everyone in the room understood.

Leaders can also use symbols to communicate new expectations for behaviour and performance. For example, you can change an expense policy or introduce a flexible work schedule to signal a culture of trust and autonomy. Additionally, you can use symbols like awards, recognition, or other incentives to encourage team members to align with the new culture.

Simply shifting away from purely individual incentives to include team incentives as part of the mix signals a move toward valuing collaboration and teamwork. Introducing sustainability or reconciliation awards indicates increased importance on carbon footprint or relationships with indigenous Australia. Announcing partnerships with community groups, or changing the criteria for grants, also symbolises a shift in direction or focus.

Stories are the most powerful symbol.

Symbols can be a powerful tool for communicating and reinforcing the culture you are trying to change. Of course, symbols alone are not enough to shift culture; actions and behaviours must back them up. Leaders need to lead by example and model the new priorities and expectations they wish to promote. They must also communicate the reasons behind the changes and be transparent and consistent.

Stories are the most powerful symbol for shaping beliefs, attitudes and behaviour.

Experiments

Try some of these experiments to recognise, design and leverage symbols in your culture:

Conduct a personal symbols audit. From your coffee mug to what you wear into the office, what you pay attention to and what messages you may inadvertently be sending.

Expand your field of view. Safety signs are symbols. Shift the impact of your next safety interaction by broadening your observations to include symbols. Look for gaps.

Borrow fresh eyes. Spend one-on-one time with a new starter in your organisation and ask about the symbols they've observed and how they interpreted them.

Mix it up. Try sitting (or parking) in a different place. In addition to a different perspective, how does this simple shift impact the dynamic in the room?

Show up loudly. Leaders wearing PPE are symbolic. Observe leaders on worksites and how 'loudly' they wear their PPE. Give positive feedback to those wearing it correctly, even if it's just what is expected on an ordinary day.

Build it and they will come. Create a new award within your team, including some kind of physical symbol. Invite your team to design the award and symbol. The process of discussing, developing and deciding is as important as the ritual of awarding the prize.

Tell the back story. Find out the brand narrative behind your organisation's logo. Practice talking about it by telling your team about the story behind the brand.

Walk in their shoes. Flex your symbology muscle by assessing your organisation's fridge etiquette or allocation of car parks. Imagine what meaning might be attributed to this and what stories might be told to a new starter.

Get out of jail free card. Give your team a get-out-of-jail-free card. You can buy cards online, but you don't need an actual printed card. The power is in the conversation. Let your team know they can come to you with any mistake, and you will work with them to solve the issue.

Reflections

What symbols exist in your workspace, desk or office? What messages might they be signalling?

What symbols do you observe onscreen of people you are meeting online?

In your next regular in-person meeting, take note of who sits where. Do people often take the same seat? Who sits at the head of the table? Where do you sit? Why?

Who plays a good symbols game that you could learn from? How do your competitors or collaborators in the marketplace use symbols?

How could you replace a symbol that doesn't align with your chosen culture? How could you do it respectfully and effectively?

10

Stories

In the 1850s, Americans came from afar to hear Abraham Lincoln, then a prairie lawyer with a gift for storytelling. Lincoln didn't have the benefit of modern technology. Standing on a tree stump, Lincoln could simultaneously educate, entertain and move his audiences.[1]

The tools we use to communicate with have changed since then, but the human brain has not. We think in narrative. We absorb and remember information in story form. Science tells us that when we listen to stories, our brains light up with the emotions experienced in the story.

Our brains are wired for stories

Understanding and creating stories is a fundamental part of human nature. We are wired for it. Stories make complex information more understandable and relatable. Studies have shown that our brains understand and remember information in a narrative format (rather than lists), which helps to make complex ideas more accessible. That is because stories provide context and emotional connection, which make information more memorable and meaningful.[2]

Stories activate different regions in our brains

When we hear a story, our brains release oxytocin, a hormone associated with social bonding and empathy. This helps us to connect emotionally with the characters in the story and understand their experiences. Stories activate different regions in our brains, such as those associated with vision, movement and emotions, as if we were experiencing the events ourselves. It makes the story more immersive and memorable.

That is why stories are often used to convey important information, such as historical events, scientific discoveries, or corporate values. By using stories, leaders make it more likely for team members to understand, remember and embrace the organisation's purpose and culture.

We need to tell our own stories. While it's engaging to describe what happened elsewhere to emphasise a point or compare and contrast with other cultures, sharing accounts about people or events in your own culture is more powerful. Stories about people we know are most effective at holding our attention. Our brains connect the story to what we already know, which means we remember.

Cultures are shared through story

Culture is passed on through storytelling. Whether morals through children's fairy tales or life lessons shared in the biography of a hero, we hand down our ways of living through stories. Stories help us make sense of the world.

The workplace is no different.

'Through stories and subsequent discussion, people collected experiences of others and accumulated knowledge of options that others had tried.'

While this observation could be made in any organisation today, it comes from an anthropologist studying the hunter-gatherer society of Ju/'hoansi (!Kung) Bushmen in southern Africa.[3] Polly Wiessner found that while the talk of the day centred on practicalities, conversations around the fire 'evoked the imagination, helped people remember and understand others in their external networks, healed rifts of the day, and conveyed information about cultural institutions that generate regularity of behaviour and corresponding trust.'[4] She found that over 85% of the evenings in this pre-industrial society were spent telling stories and sharing myths.[5] Stories might have changed medium and media today, but they still hold power.

Stories help us make sense of the world.

In Australia, we have so much to learn from indigenous communities and the role of storytelling in sustaining the world's longest continuous culture. It is important to acknowledge and honour the role of storytelling in Australian Aboriginal culture and its significance in passing on knowledge and culture for tens of thousands of years.

Brad Twynham, indigenous leader, Guringai and Awabakal man of the Wanganini (Saltwater) people of the Central Coast of NSW, says storytelling is the original classroom where history, morality and knowledge about people, places and the world are relayed to each new generation.

'Every business today is focused on creating an enduring and engaging culture. For over 60,000 years, our people have used stories to organise data, share information, pass down lore (rules, obligations, protocols and lessons), and make sense of the world. Our songlines and storylines connected nations and tribes across Australia and gave a common understanding, even though we spoke different languages and dialects. Story made it possible for us to connect, trade and learn and was the central thread that made Australian Aboriginal culture the most enduring, continuous culture on earth.'[6]

In *Sand Talk*, Tyson Yunkaporta discusses the importance of Dreamtime and storytelling in Australian Aboriginal culture.[7] According to Yunkaporta, Dreamtime stories are not only creation myths; they hold practical knowledge and wisdom that can be applied to everyday life. He argues that the Dreamtime stories are a form of information technology passed down through generations, enabling indigenous Australians to adapt to their environment and sustain their culture for tens of thousands of years.

Yunkaporta's writing process begins with images. Honouring indigenous traditions, he makes carvings of what he wants to say, channelling his thoughts through symbols rather than words. He yarns with people, looking for ways to connect images and stories with place and relationship to create a coherent worldview and uses sand talk, the Aboriginal custom of drawing images on the ground, to convey knowledge.

His book emphasises the role of storytelling, explaining that stories are not just entertainment; they transmit knowledge and teach important lessons about community, relationships, and the natural world. Dreamtime and stories connect people to their history, ancestors and land, creating a sense of belonging and identity central to indigenous culture.

Culture is shared through stories. They are a powerful tool for transmitting cultural values and beliefs within an organisation and across generations. They create a sense of shared identity and purpose among team members and provide a way for them to connect with and understand the organisation's purpose and culture.

Stories are sticky

Sharing stories connects and engages us. They are a powerful tool for transmitting culture and creating shared identity and purpose.

Leaders use stories to communicate organisational history and culture and share information about the organisation's purpose, products, services, or industry. Stories tell of an organisation's successes and challenges, providing team members with a sense of context and perspective. For example, a family business may use stories to pass down the organisation's purpose and culture from one generation to the next.

Dan Gregory, speaker, author and social commentator, says he's always inspired by how resilient stories are, especially

Sharing stories connects and engages us.

when they define the parameters of a culture. 'A catch-up with a co-worker from 20 years ago will often elicit a retelling of the same stories, over and over, because they exemplify the culture and the experience of the time. These stories are best when they are personal, portable, shareable and re-tellable. They have values built in and can use humour as an anaesthetic when emotions run high and conflict is rising.'[8]

Stories answer the question 'Why do things work this way here?'

Origin stories

Do you know how Peter Parker became Spiderman? Do you know why Bruce Wayne became Batman? What about Wonder Woman? Do you know where her strength, stamina and intelligence come from? Or her golden lasso of truth? Maybe superheroes aren't your thing. Do you know the story of Mozart's rise to fame? Or how the cricketer Don Bradman got started?

Hollywood loves an origin story. So do team members.

As an organisation grows and evolves, it can be easy to lose sight of the original purpose. An origin story is typically a narrative that provides a glimpse into the organisation's history and how it has evolved. It is a reminder of why the organisation was founded and what it stands for. It provides context for your organisation's purpose and principles and typically positions the founder, or founders, as heroes of the story.

Origin stories can be a powerful tool for creating a sense of shared identity and purpose among team members. When team members understand the reasons behind your organisation's purpose, they are more likely to be engaged and motivated in their work and focus on what matters most. Additionally, an origin story can help communicate your culture to current and potential team members, making attracting and retaining top talent easier.

Origin stories can serve as a cultural anchor, fostering a sense of community and belonging and reminding team members of the purpose and values in times of change or uncertainty. Stories connect team members to the organisation and each other, which is especially important for remote or dispersed teams, who have fewer opportunities to bond in person.

So, take the time to craft a compelling origin story that reflects your purpose and culture and share it with your team members and customers regularly.

Despite its size and global reach, Marriott International remains a family business. When I worked there, the chairman, Bill Marriott, made a point of communicating

Take the time to craft a compelling origin story.

that regularly to team members. I still remember the story he told me when I met him in London, of counting sticky nickels at night as a child. These were the proceeds from the root-beer stand founded in downtown Washington DC by his mother and father. His humility, his values of hard work and family, and the fact that he had worked his way through the organisation resonated then and stick with me today.

Yet beware the cult of the founder. When crafting your origin story, balance the role of the founder with the team and the evolution of the organisation. It's tempting to set up founders as inviolable heroes and over-inflate their role. Heritage provides a solid basis for your origin story, but it's vital to look beyond the superhero narrative.

Reliance on a legend as the only part of the origin story leaves organisations vulnerable to the foibles of flawed humans. Weave in humility or share lessons learned from setbacks and failures. This shifts your origin story from a potentially ego-led legend to something that engages the audience by humanising the founders.

Importantly, this leaves room for team members to contribute to the ongoing story.

Nostalgia plays an interesting role in organisations. Often, the way things were, is held up as an ideal to return to. And sometimes, our attachment to the past affects our ability to accept change and move rapidly to the new. In his 2021 Harvard Business Review article, *The Surprising Power of Nostalgia at Work*, Clay Routledge shared his findings after 20 years of research on nostalgia.[9] He says people use nostalgia naturally and frequently to navigate stress and uncertainty and find the motivation to move forward with purpose and focus. Like rituals, stories from the past activate nostalgia.

It's important to remember that you cannot control the stories told about your organisation, your culture or your leadership. While the organisation might share curated stories, the myths and legends about heroes and villains that flow through your culture shape it like a glacier cutting through a mountain.

Myths, legends, heroes and villains

Organisational myths and legends, heroes and villains, play a crucial role in shaping workplace culture. By identifying with the heroes and legends, team members feel connected to the organisation and each other. Recognising and celebrating the achievements of team members who embody the organisation's values helps create a sense of pride and belonging among your workforce.

Whenever I join a new organisation or team, I soak up the stories. I love hearing the tales from decades ago, marvelling at how the industry and organisations have changed. Stories of old miners wearing shorts and thongs while operating draglines stand in sharp contrast to the safety gear and personal protective equipment that are standard today. It's always a privilege to listen to an elder in a culture share stories from former times.

Pictures tell stories too. The picture wall at 3M's Sydney offices depicts key innovations throughout the company's history. Similarly, the entrance to Blackwoods' offices has photos covering its 140-year history, highlighting the number of smaller brands and family businesses combined over time into the industrial and safety supplies giant it is today. AAMI Insurance employed a librarian to manage its historical archives until 2010, when the content was largely digitalised.

Pictures tell stories too.

Myths and legends typically communicate the organisation's history, purpose and priorities. Like origin stories, they act as a reminder of the founding purpose and ways of working in times of change or uncertainty. Sharing myths and legends create a sense of belonging and community among team members and provide a shared narrative and history.

Heroes and villains are representative of what matters most to the organisation. Where heroes represent the ideals the organisation aspires to, villains symbolise the opposite. By highlighting the actions and beliefs of heroes, the organisation can communicate the behaviours and values it wants to encourage among team members. The actions and beliefs of villains serve to discourage and warn people of what is unacceptable in the culture and, often, the consequences of not doing the right thing. Other than founders, stories of heroes and villains are typically from today or the recent past. Occasionally, people leave a legacy, and their story is told well beyond their time in the organisation.

When working with organisations, I talk about my (yet-to-be-invented) cloning machine. It helps when we talk about cultural role models. I ask: Who are the heroes that demonstrate our desired ways of working? What do they do that makes you want more of them? What is it about them that makes you wish cloning had been invented? It is a bit of fun but helps break down the barriers that sometimes emerge at this point. We can be reluctant to nominate people as heroes.

Once we break the hero barrier, the names come quickly. Over a series of interviews, some people will be named many times. While these are essential for my process (we always try to interview some of the heroes), what I'm listening for is *why* people are nominated. What is it about them that people see as exemplifying the culture? It tells me what is valued and provides colour and real-life examples of cultural performance norms. Think about who you would name in your culture. Why? What is it about those people that make them heroes? Is that articulated as valued, or is it unwritten?

Stories make it stick

We all need to share more stories of success and what good looks like.

Too frequently, when assessing cultures, I find that crucial messages are not getting through to the frontline, even when leaders are convinced that they are regularly communicating positive news. The marketing world uses the rule of seven to guide how often to repeat a message, but this is from the 1930s. Imagine how many times we need to repeat something to cut through all the noise surrounding us now. Certainly, one or two repetitions will not be enough.

Stories help with memorability and shareability, but leaders must still repeat key messages. Tell the story again. Share it with different audiences. Tell a different story to underline the same point. Increasing the number of stories told increases the likelihood of the message cutting through. In fact, keep telling stories until they start being shared back with you.

By sharing stories about organisational successes and team wins, you signal to your teams what matters, what good looks like and what you'd like more of. When you tell stories about how teams win, you share ways of working and what is working well, enabling organisational learning. What you focus on and pay attention to in your storytelling indicates to the listeners what your priorities are.

> Share stories about your priorities and the stories behind them.

Leaders need to share stories from the past and the present and tell stories of the future. Bring your vision to life with stories about what it will be like. Help show people the future through the use of stories. Look for opportunities to thread the past, present and future together.

It's also important to share stories about your priorities and the stories behind them. What matters, and why it matters.

When things aren't going well

Our brains are wired for story, but also focused on threats and keeping us safe. Look at what media sells best.

More often than not, my diagnostic assessing culture highlights that leaders are focused on what is going wrong — not what is going right. This approach leads to a downward spiral. It's a vicious cycle. When performance is dropping, it's even more important to focus on what is going well and what good looks like. Shift the dialogue to a virtuous cycle. Keep your team focused on the big and the few. Narrowing your focus is vital to shift performance; stories can help you achieve this.

Farewells can also provide a moment of truth. What stories are told about someone when they are leaving or have left your organisation? What stories do you tell? Like farewell rituals, these stories can serve or actively work against your chosen culture. Does resigning instantly turn someone into a villain? Is someone previously regarded as a hero now painted as someone with stinky clay feet? A positive or negative experience on the way out the door creates its own story stack. Combine this with the recency effect, and now your former team member shares stories with future teammates and potential talent about their last days. What stories would you like them to be sharing?

As a heavily regulated industry, coal mining has developed clear practices about sharing the story of all high-potential incidents and fatalities. In Queensland, there is a requirement to report each incident, and external inspections occur. There is usually a very swift turnaround for the initial report and findings.

Every miner across the state starts their shift by listening to the safety bulletins detailing what occurred and what the lessons were. This is in addition to any local safety issues, minor incidents or changes to conditions that have occurred since their last shift. While the mine site is named in the bulletins, the stories are otherwise anonymised – each person is named as a mine worker, supervisor or inspector.

This might sound clinical, but for operators about to head out on shift, it can feel very real. When an incident results in a fatality, the mood is sombre and heartfelt, even if they don't know the individuals involved. Counselling is available for miners for whom the story brings back past incidents. The system ensures each story is shared across the industry. It's a powerful example of learning from examples.

Redemption stories

Stories of redemption are prevalent in most cultures, from Charles Dicken's fictional character, Scrooge, to the real-life remorseful bullfighter, Alvaro Munera, who now campaigns for animal rights. Most popular fiction involves redemption arcs which typically follow the hero's journey, as articulated by Joseph Campbell.

Redemption stories are powerful ways of sharing unacceptable behaviour and the path back to belonging. They convey social and cultural norms, the consequences of breaking them and how to make restitution to return to acceptance. Some of the most potent examples of personal stories shifting behaviour have been people taking accountability for wrongdoing, apologising, and sharing the impact of the behaviour on themselves and those around them.

> Redemption stories are powerful ways of sharing unacceptable behaviour and the path back to belonging.

While working at a mine site in central Queensland, I was privileged to witness such a story. An up-and-coming supervisor (let's call him

Dave) was hauled in to show cause why he shouldn't face immediate dismissal. Dave had been reported for using racist slurs on the radio, on a channel heard by several crews working onsite the day before. As a local guy whose father had also worked on the site, Dave was well-liked by the crews and his peers. The behaviour felt out of step with how he normally presented himself. A peer reported him, but others had raised concerns about his language.

We conducted an investigation, including interviewing Dave and the teammate, Jim, with whom he'd used the language. Dave and Jim were friends outside of work, and Jim did not want to raise a formal complaint against Dave. Dave admitted he had used racial slurs on the radio but said he'd just been joking around and that was how he always spoke with Jim. Jim said he often used those words about himself and didn't want Dave to be punished. Initially, Dave and Jim were only sorry that they had been overheard in what was meant to be a private conversation.

It only took Dave five minutes in the general manager's office before he realised just how wrong he'd been. The GM and I walked him through systemic racism, how impacted people take on language as a pre-emptive defence mechanism and that his language was beyond acceptable. His growing horror and contrition were genuine. He accepted he faced dismissal for his behaviour. In accordance with our policy, we gave Dave 24 hours to respond with why he should not be dismissed for his actions.

The following day, Dave apologised. He accepted whatever decision we made but wanted to make amends, including a public apology across all crews onsite. We accepted his offer. He was demoted but returned to work. He proposed and delivered one of the most heartfelt and impactful anti-racism campaigns I have seen. In addition to apologising to Jim and other teammates he knew he'd used similar language with, Dave shared his story.

Dave told his story more than 20 times in front of his peers and leaders. He shared his actions and his learning. Dave spoke of his deep regret and how carelessly and casually he'd used slurs. He apologised to all and committed publicly to ceasing his use of that language and calling out anyone who did.

You could hear a pin drop each time Dave spoke with the crews. This was one of their own sharing a deeply personal learning. Language that had been commonplace in the town pubs shifted from that week to the next. Dave agreed to record his story on video, and it became part of the on-site respectful workplace training program. His genuine remorse and commitment to making a difference was a powerful redemption story that rippled out of the workplace and into the local community.

Organisations are full of stories, but are they the stories you want?

Playground or playbook stories

Penny Terry is a communications expert who specialises in workplace and community storytelling. She says two types of stories tend to shape the culture of an organisation — playground or playbook stories.[10]

Playground stories tell on others. *Playbook* stories show others how.

Playground stories are about people. They give airtime to assumptions, opinions and gossip. They tend to be a catalyst for unhelpful narratives. They often start with 'Did you hear...?', 'I can't believe...', 'Guess what...', 'Why did you...?'

Playbook stories are all about action. They help us see new ways to work and get things done by connecting the personal to the universal. They become a common language that allows us to explain what our values look like day-to-day. They often end with significant learning.

Playground stories	Playbook stories
About people	About action
Create chaos	Create community
Catalyst for division	Catalyst for connection
Encourage gossip	Encourage thinking
Created from hurt	Created to help
Highlight difference	Highlight similarity

This week, listen to the stories being told around you. Reflect on the stories you're sharing. Are they playground or playbook stories?

I remember when people believed messages in organisations could be controlled. Certainly, gossip and the rumour mill existed, but official messaging was managed through official spokespeople. Communication was handled via hierarchy. Messages took days and sometimes weeks to be drafted and approved before being shared in a cascade fashion. Big announcements were communicated to the media, ready for publication the following day. There was a sense of controlling the release of content and the timing of the message.

Corporate affairs teams work very differently today.

The evolution of social media and online news has accelerated the speed of communication and seen a fracturing of audience, message and sources. Now team members can learn about organisational changes from social media hours before official communication hits them. Adjustments have been made.

As a conglomerate, Wesfarmers has created an environment where multiple cultures co-exist in harmony, with an underpinning core of Wesfarmers' culture. Openness and integrity are two of the four values. One of the key cultural tenets shared across all Wesfarmers businesses is that *bad news travels faster than good news*. My boss told me this on my first day as he welcomed and oriented me in my new role.

During my ten years in multiple roles, he and every other leader I reported to frequently repeated this mantra. It was repeated whenever I reported an incident or shared a concern. It was repeated whenever discussions were held about risks or potential issues. I saw it used as a guiding light for making decisions by operational supervisors and warehouse managers, sales and technical teams, and equally for legal and financial teams. I saw it modelled by the two group managing directors during their tenure.

Better than bush telegraph

I will never forget working with police and authorities to contact family members following fatalities at work, racing against time to let people know before they found out from social media or the grapevine. News travels fast over the bush telegraph in small country towns and related industries. My team and I balanced the need for privacy, respect and compassion while also trying to respond to concerns from colleagues and their families.

When emotions are high, getting the message right is even more essential. Who delivers the message and how it is delivered are incredibly symbolic. The cultural ramifications of the actions of leaders at times like these are significant. Every word is replayed.

When I arrived at my new job on a mine site in 2013, it was the fifth anniversary of someone killed at work. In my first week, I was told multiple stories about what had happened, how the mineworker was remembered, and the support provided to his family. Stories about the incident response and aftermath. Stories of how the crew had been impacted and how they'd come together as a workforce. Story after story of the unofficial support given to the family and the strength of connection that emerged. It gave me a real insight into what mattered most at this organisation; its very real commitment to safety, family and community.

Aside from today's greater speed and demand for information, this shift saw communication within organisations shift from hierarchy to wirearchy.[11] This concept, developed by Jon Husband, heavily influenced me when I first read about it in 2005. Jon showed how changes in information flow and greater interconnection fundamentally shift leadership and organisations.

> *'Today's rapid flows of information are like electronic grains of sand, eroding the pillars of rigid traditional hierarchies. This new set of conditions is having real impact on organizational structures and the dynamics these structures generate, contain and also block. In turn, this impact is growing into massive change in the ways we do things and behave.'[12]*

I have seen Jon's predictions unfold in the nearly 20 years since.

The resulting increased transparency has led to greater accountability. Power dynamics have shifted in small and large ways. Jon believes leaders need to become aware of interconnected markets and flows of information. He suggests leaders understand how and why people connect, talk and share information, and be prepared to listen deeply, be responsible, accountable and transparent.

How do you consume information differently today than when you first learned to lead? Think about the stories told then and now about leaders (good and bad). How have they changed?

Bullet points don't shift culture

'I have come to realise that most culture transformation efforts fail when we focus too much on leading these changes with facts and figures rather than embracing stories which create an emotional response.'
— Gabrielle Dolan.[13]

Facts inform, while stories influence.[14] Facts provide information and data that we can use to make decisions and understand the world around us. They are logical, objective and verifiable. However, facts alone are not always enough to change behaviour or attitudes.

Stories are a powerful tool for influencing our thoughts and emotions. They provide context and emotional connection, which helps make information more memorable and meaningful. Through stories, we can put ourselves in someone else's shoes and understand their experiences and perspectives, which can change attitudes and behaviour.

Facts provide information that we can use to make decisions. However, stories are a powerful tool for influencing our thoughts and emotions. They give context and emotional connection, making complex information more relatable and understandable.

By using a combination of facts and stories, leaders can effectively communicate their message and influence the thoughts and actions of others.

A bulleted list is not a story.

Gianna DiBella, the co-founder of DiBella Group, works with their CFO to report figures and also to tell a story with the figures. For example, she says, 'We are transparent about our monthly and annual revenue and report the figures. Then we tell the story that we served five million cups of coffee and helped 40 start-up roasters realise their dream of starting their own business. We are all emotional beings, and this is what connects with our team and our customers.'[15]

A bulleted list is not a story. A story is a series of events told through words and, now more than ever, pictures. Stories are powerful tools for shaping culture, providing context and emotional connection and making team members more likely to embrace and act upon them. A story has a theme, attention-grabbing moments, heroes and villains, and a satisfying conclusion.

Bullet points may be a concise and convenient way to convey information, but they are ineffective in shifting culture. They are dry and lack the emotional connection that stories provide. That makes it more difficult for team members to understand the importance of your culture and less likely to remember or commit to action.

Stories create a sense of shared identity and purpose among team members, fostering a sense of belonging and community. They allow team members to hear and see firsthand how your organisation's culture is implemented, which helps to create a sense of ownership and pride. Fact-based communication is often abstract and disconnected from the day-to-day experiences of team members, making it difficult for team members to see its relevance to their work.

Downer Professional Services (DPS) provides multi-disciplinary advisory and delivery to clients, including government, defence and infrastructure.[16] The nature of their work on critical, nation-building and security projects attracts many veterans from the Australian Defence Force. The meaningful employment of veterans post-transition is a cause I am passionate about.

DPS uses the power of stories from team members who are veterans to normalise some of the early transition experiences of new team members. One veteran shared with me that after 20 years of grabbing his hat to walk into work in the army, he still reached for it as he pulled into the car park at DPS or client offices. These kinds of stories help new starters deal with their personal concerns.

Outside onboarding, DPS uses videos of team members telling stories of their career paths and progression through the organisation. This has proven effective and empowering for defence force veterans, whose careers were managed for them. Candid stories of team members making mistakes and the responses they experienced have also dismantled myths about how the private sector managed performance. These videos have become cultural assets for DPS as they onboard and orient veterans, and other new team members, into their culture.

Hearing others' experiences helps team members better understand how culture and values play out in real-life situations. Bullet points work for simple facts but are often too general or lack the perspective that helps team members

Facts may inform us, but stories move us.

to make decisions where discretion is required. Humans are used to learning how to behave through stories. We naturally absorb the context and perspective when stories of successes and challenges are shared.

We want to tell inspiring, motivating stories that foster a sense of shared identity and purpose among team members. We want to tell stories that shift us closer to our chosen culture. To promote innovation and creativity, share stories of team members who have taken risks and come up with new and creative solutions. To encourage teamwork and collaboration, share stories of team members who have worked together to achieve a common goal.

Remember, facts may inform us, but stories move us.

The stories we share

What's the story?

Do you know what stories are being told in your team? What stories would you like to be told? As leaders, we need to be aware of which stories are circulating as these shape the culture and impact attitudes and behaviours. To know what people are saying, ask team members for their perspectives and listen to their feedback. Observe the interactions and communication among team members and look for emerging patterns and themes.

> Notice which stories resonate and are repeated.

The meaning attributed to stories

matters more than the stories themselves. The same set of facts can be interpreted in many ways. Sharing your perspective can help reshape stories so they are more aligned with your chosen culture – or what actually happened.

Listen up

We learn to *listen* to stories before we learn to *tell* them, so start your storytelling journey as a leader by listening. What stories are being told in your organisation today? Listen to what is said and what is unsaid. Notice which stories resonate and are repeated. Listen for the lessons and cultural messages shared in the subtext.

What's your story?

Develop your own stories. Collect and curate stories as they occur around you or as you hear them. Create a system to capture, store and access your stories.

Shawn Callahan, the author of *Putting Stories to Work*, says leaders tell four kinds of stories.[17]

- Connection stories build rapport fast
- Clarity stories explain why something is happening
- Influence stories change people's minds
- Success stories share achievements at a human level.

Sometimes you have a great story but need to connect it to a point. Using a simple story structure makes crafting and sharing stories easier. As the saying goes, no point should be made without a story, and no story should be made without a point.

Jason Thompson works with leaders to build confidence, clarity and conviction through strategic storytelling. He says, 'Stories have the power to change the world because they connect with people on an emotional level that inspires action. When you own your story and share it with confidence, clarity and conviction you will enhance attention, create anticipation and increase the retention of your message.'[18]

The most powerful stories a leader can share draw out their vulnerability. And leaders showing vulnerability have more impact on a team's psychological safety than any other action. Stories are a great place to start.

By being open, honest and transparent about your own experiences, failures and struggles, you create a sense of trust and relatability, foster a culture of openness and honesty, build empathy and understanding, and encourage a culture of growth and learning. Leaders need to be comfortable sharing their vulnerabilities, be role models for their team members and inspire them to do the same.

> Defn: Vulnerability is the ability to be open, honest and transparent about your own experiences, failures and struggles.

Sharing stories of vulnerability humanises leaders and makes them more approachable. It allows team members to see that their leaders are not infallible and that they, too, have faced and overcome challenges. This promotes a culture of openness and honesty, where team members feel comfortable sharing their struggles and learning from each other.

Change strategist Emma Gibbens reminds us that if you expect others to share stories, you must first share a story. She says, 'People will match the level of vulnerability and openness you bring, so you need to model it.' Vulnerability builds empathy and understanding among team members. They can see that their leaders understand their challenges and care about their well-being. That knowledge creates a culture of support and teamwork, where team members feel motivated to work together to overcome challenges.

Vulnerability stories support a culture of growth and learning, where team members feel encouraged to take risks and learn from their mistakes. When you share your experiences of failure and how you overcame them, you offer perspective, inspiration and even permission, for people to learn from their mistakes.

> **Create a culture where people feel safe to tell their stories.**

Everyone has a story

How can you create a culture where people feel safe to tell their stories?

Leading by example and integrating storytelling into your leadership is a great place to start creating a culture of storytelling. Tell your personal stories, particularly those that share your vulnerability. Ask for stories in meetings. Safety shares, where people tell a story related to their personal safety or something they observed with a lesson worth sharing, are a great way to set the tone. One of the reasons safety shares work as a behavioural nudge is that team members listen to and share their own stories. Rather than starting every meeting with a PowerPoint that says 'Safety Matters', stories are engaging, authentic and remind people to keep safety front of mind.

What makes a good story?

Penny Terry says great stories are simple, specific and about single moments. These make stories memorable and repeatable, leading to shifts in behaviour and perspectives.[19]

> **Brains prefer stories about things rather than complex ideas.**

Don't overcomplicate your stories. Keep them simple. Often the best stories are made up of a simple, relatable experience with a profound statement to match. Simple stories can be told in minutes. Focusing on a single person, a moment or an event helps our brain absorb the meaning. Brains prefer stories about things rather than complex ideas. The more statistics or bullet points, the less we care.

Make it real. Use concrete details people can picture to cement their memory. Being specific reduces ambiguity, misunderstanding and assumptions. These details also help a story be repeatable, which is vital to shifting culture.

Media personality and executive Oprah Winfrey is known for her ability to connect with her audience and build emotional engagement through stories. She has used storytelling throughout her career to create a sense of empathy and understanding among her audience. Oprah's 2018 Golden Globes speech was a masterclass in using stories with a point, to be impactful and memorable.[20] In eight minutes, she delivered an inspiring and compelling moment.

Putting aside her skill in delivery, look for these three tips.

Make it balanced. Seek opposites and place them next to each other. We naturally compare. When you share a story about your newest team member, pair it with a story about a veteran team member. When you share a story about your greatest success, connect it to a story of your biggest failure. Comparing and contrasting makes each part stronger and resonate more.

Make it lyrical. Look for rhythm and repeat yourself. Repeating a key phrase isn't boring if it's done well. It's the best way to make something memorable. It helps to have a memorable mantra or call to action you can repeat.

Make it personal. Think about the most impactful stories you've heard. They all involved some hurt or pain. Lean in. Don't gloss over it because the pain is where the power is. It sets up the other side of the story. And when delivering, don't hold back your emotional reactions because they give permission for others to share in the emotions.

So, collect and share your stories. Encourage others to embrace storytelling.

Get better at telling stories. Practise out loud.

Remember, bullet points and PowerPoints don't shift culture. Stories do.

> 'Every story begins inside a story that's already begun
> by others. Long before we take our first breath, there's
> a plot underway, with characters and a setting we
> did not choose, but which were chosen for us.'
> — **Richard Blanco**[21]

Experiments

There are several ways to start to build your storytelling capability, understand your culture through stories and build a culture of storytelling. Try some of these experiments.

Assess your culture's stories. Adam Grant suggests asking three kinds of stories of current team members to assess a culture before accepting a job offer.[22]

- Stories about something that happens here that wouldn't elsewhere
- Stories about when people didn't walk the talk
- Stories about who gets hired, promoted or fired.

These are a good place to start. What would these stories be in your organisation?

Share personal stories. Leaders can share their own stories, experiences and lessons learned to provide context and emotional connection to the organisation's purpose and priorities. Share them in team meetings, organisation-wide events and through video or written communications.

Encourage team member storytelling. Leaders can create opportunities for team members to share their stories and experiences. Try storytelling sessions where team members can share their stories or an organisation-wide storytelling contest where team members can submit stories that align with the culture and priorities.

Use storytelling to promote learning. Weave stories from a diverse range of leaders and team members into learning and development programs to make the material more relatable and memorable. Use video, case studies, role-playing, or other interactive storytelling methods.

Use storytelling to profile teams. Use storytelling to connect across siloes within your organisation. By profiling teams and individual team members, you can highlight the great work happening in different areas. Break down silos by increasing understanding of what each area does and who works in those teams. Use team member testimonials externally to promote your culture to prospective talent. Share case studies, wins, wobbles and other stories to show how the teams have positively impacted customers and the community.

Incorporate storytelling into your culture. Create a storytelling culture by encouraging storytelling sessions, competitions, or other forums that give opportunities for team members to share their stories and experiences. Reward teams and team members that share stories. Create a double loop reinforcing the power of stories by telling the story of the impact storytelling has on their team.

Reflections

What's your go-to story? Do you have one about learning, one about leading and one that leads to laughter?

What's your connection story?

What stories would you like shared about your team? About your leadership?

What stories are told about your organisation's origin? The founders?

Who are the heroes and villains in your culture's stories, past and present?

What myths and legends are retold? Do they reinforce the culture of the past? Could they reinforce your chosen culture?

How rampant is the rumour mill? What stories are being told at the proverbial water cooler? How do they differ from reality?

Are you telling playground or playbook stories? Which are your team telling?

Who are the best storytellers in your culture? How can you raise the visibility of storytellers?

How could you encourage storytelling in your team?

Part 3

Hitting the Ground Running

The Story Behind Hitting the Ground Running

Coffee and change seem to be strong threads throughout my career.

I earned my white belt in change in my late teens, working as one of the first baristas in Brisbane and experiencing the birth of coffee culture. There were very few espresso machines in Brisbane back then. One of my first waiting jobs in a café on Park Rd in Milton saw me flown to Sydney to attend barista training. It was a big deal for someone fresh out of school and in my first year at university. I think I was chosen because I knew the difference between a cappuccino and a flat white. Until then, you could only find 'cuppachinos' (filter coffee served with whipped cream and chocolate sprinkles) in David Jones or Myers' city stores. Or you might order an Irish coffee with dessert as the height of sophistication.

My manager and I were to train my teammates to make coffee on a real espresso machine. Back then, the coffee machine installed in the café cost more than my car. I had to wrangle my fear of it before I could help my colleagues manage theirs. It was my first lesson in fear and resistance to change in the workplace. I learned the hard way that fear of change got in the way of learning, even simple tasks.

I earned my green belt in change shifting Marriott hotels in the UK, Europe, North Africa and the Middle East from brand-standard American drip filter coffee to espresso coffee. Imagine, if you will, an Aussie representing an American approach and delivering the accompanying training, in countries with coffee traditions older than my federated nation.

I was on the pointy end of the change working with hotel leadership teams, food and beverage teams and front office teams to shift equipment, menus and service to serve espresso coffee in all hotels. Given local preferences, most properties already had some version available onsite, so the change was often standardisation rather than an introduction.

There were many instances when this proved harder than it might have been to introduce something new. And it took a lot of coffee – and some metaphorical tap dancing shoes – to deliver the requisite 'how to make a coffee' training with a straight face, and in an engaging way, to my colleagues who had all been drinking 'real' coffee for generations. My green belt came with an expensive coffee habit.

My black belt in change was earned through the GFC. After a brutal season in financial services leading organisational change and redundancies associated with an acquisition cum merger, I rolled straight into successive downsizing resulting from the GFC. Over a two-year period from 2007 to 2009, my team and I held thousands of redundancy conversations.

When I see media reporting on job losses and the impacted employees, I always spare a thought for the team that made the decisions and delivered the outcome conversations with people. There were a lot of late nights and early morning coffees. Lots of coffees with leaders making changes, impacted people who needed a coffee to come to terms with the outcome and debriefing over coffee with my team. By the end of that period, I had earned a commercial PhD in human behaviour, change and culture – and my doctor advised me to give up coffee.

In the decade 2010-2020, my black belt in change never got dusty. I was attracted to the meatiest change agendas and fortunate enough to partner with courageous leaders willing to push the boat out. I've led teams and organisations through rapid growth and acquisitions, downturns, turnarounds and transformations across industries ranging from financial services to manufacturing and mining. The greater the complexity, the more opportunity to work with great people and find creative solutions. I loved big change. I learned all change is behaviour change. I cemented my belief that all change is cultural change.

> All change is cultural change.

And I learned to love tea.

When I made the decision to leave my corporate career and do my own thing, I knew I wanted to work differently. I didn't have firm views on what I would focus on, but I knew I wanted to do work I loved. I wanted to take my time to explore what leaders needed over the first few months and see what evolved from there.

Over the course of three months, I had 100 coffee meetings. I caught up with former colleagues and friends. I met with leaders from a variety of industries and sectors. The conversations over those coffees ranged from comforting to confronting and inspired me to focus on culture. These first two years in business have been remarkable. I have learned so much and am grateful for the opportunities to do great work with great people.

You might have noticed that I have used the word change more in this short section than in the entire book. That's because I have worked hard to remove change (and transformation) from my vocabulary. Over the years, I might have overdosed on those two words (and coffee). I'm also cautious about using language like 'end state' and 'destination' (and journey!).

I now deliberately use words like shifting and moving instead.

I've learned that working one-on-one with the executive to shift their leadership can have as great an impact as hundreds of leaders attending a training program.

I've also learned to surf the wave rather than swim against the tide. To use the existing cultures to springboard toward the new. To go where the energy is and work with those who want to change first. To start before you start and strengthen as you go.

I've learned the grass is greenest where you water it. To share idea generation, plant seeds and allow time for them to germinate. Nurture the seedlings and green shoots. That time invested up front is always worth it. As my mates in mining would say, go slow to go fast.

> **Start before you start and strengthen as you go.**

I've learned that the lure of sunshine is more powerful than any bulldozing push. And that a groundswell of momentum can become unstoppable. That grassroots change combined with water and sunshine achieves the most sustainable outcomes.

I've learned that while big change is powerful and necessary, unless it is accompanied by real, every day and tangible shifts, it won't stick.

And I've learned there is nothing like hitting the ground running.

Hitting the Ground Running

We've covered a lot of ground in these pages. We've explored what culture is and why it is important. We worked through five everyday areas of focus you can action as a leader, including gatherings, rituals, actions, symbols and stories.

Ready, set, go

It's time to develop your game plan.

Using the reflection questions at the end of the GRASS chapters (six through ten), consider where you need to focus your most urgent attention.

Decide which experiments you wish to start with.

> It's time to develop your game plan.

Gather your allies, whether they are your team, your peers, your leader or your support crew in the people and culture team.

Get started and use the deliberate practice model to make the most of your learning when experimenting.

Get the culture conversation going.

Blur the starting line

If you're in a room with me on a retreat or leadership development program, you might arrive 15 minutes early to see people already scribbling or reading. I'm a fan of a rolling start to workshops. I always provide an option to start before the start. Of course, these activities are usually reflective or conversational ones that help warm people up and smoothly transition into the workshop. It's not school – there is no need for me to ring a bell to signal the start of the day.

Over the years, my teams have been frustrated with me wanting to start before the start.

I admit to being impatient. I have an aversion to waterfall change. I've seen the success of viral change, and I can't unsee it. Activator is one of my top five Gallup strengths. In fact, my top two strengths are Strategic and Futuristic, followed by Individualisation and then Activator. For me, the future is vividly clear and palpable, and so are the paths to get there. I naturally personalise and tailor experiences for each person as an individual. My Activator means I want to get started. And I want to start where the energy is.

Hitting the ground running means you are starting the change before you officially start the change. The starting line is blurred.

When I work with organisations, one of the first steps in the Cultureshift program is to assess the culture. I report on culture strengths and shadows and the required shifts. Equally important is how we interact with and engage team members through the discovery and diagnostic process. How we talk about culture in conversations shapes how people start to think about and talk about culture.

The very process of asking about culture is an opportunity to educate or engage everyone who participates. Asking leaders and team members about what is working and what is not, can make explicit people's niggles or giggles. How we talk about the work — announcing the process (or not) and inviting people to participate in culture conversations one-on-one or in focus groups — all contribute to the success of the diagnostic but, more importantly, the coming culture shift. Even asking people to think about culture in order to respond to a culture survey is starting a ripple effect that can become a culture wave if managed well.

The best way to shift culture is to be culturally aligned in how you do the change.

Don't sit around a leadership team table and agree that the culture will empower your team members. It's hypocritical and will kill, or slow considerably, the shifts you wish to make in your culture. Rather, gather a selection of your best and brightest to co-create your culture. The more aspirational you can make the experience for your chosen team members, the more buzz you will generate. This buzz contributes to the anticipation across your teams about culture and creates the conditions for momentum.

Craft an experience for your design team that previews the culture. While we might not know the nuances of the culture you desire, we can probably be confident that working together collaboratively in respectful and creative ways wouldn't be out of place in your new culture. Like a greenhouse, we want to nurture and protect the delicate culture seedlings at this point, so care and the right conditions matter.

Notice, I haven't started at the beginning, stepping through the decision to work on culture, selecting your partner or if you need to produce a business case to do so. I'm writing on the assumption that you have prepped the ground and fertilised the soil with the board and key stakeholders.

If you aren't running a relay, with organisation-wide culture work underway around you, the same principles apply.

In your team, make some shifts and try some experiments before you start talking about culture. Once you start these conversations, you are on your way. Some shifts are better back-announced, like a 1990s classic rock radio station. Help people recognise the changes you've introduced after you've made some. Provide context and motivation after you've tried things out and ask for feedback to tailor at that point. Recognise that inviting your team to join your crusade to create capacity by meeting better, shifts culture before you make any changes to your meetings. Including your team in the design of a team ritual to strengthen your culture is, in itself, shifting your culture.

From your team members' perspective, you haven't started the culture shift. You are still working out what the culture will be. Yet the buzz has started. The starting line is blurred. You have started before the start.

The sprint

Even with unlimited resources to shift all your culture's systems, frameworks, symbols and scaffolding, your organisation has a limited capacity to absorb change. So, how do you focus your efforts on the things that matter most? And where do you start?

While we certainly need to redesign systems, frameworks, tools and practices at an organisational level to scaffold the culture, to sustain change, leaders need to shift how they and their teams work every day.

Front and centre of any successful shift are leaders. The best starting point is investing in leader behaviours and getting leaders invested in the culture shift. Leaders bring the multiplier effect, whether it is the CEO and executive team leading the organisation or managers leading their teams.

The formula is:

Moments that matter x Multipliers = Chosen culture

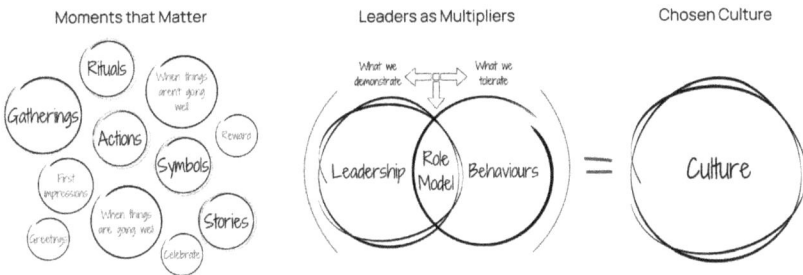

The next step is to understand the current culture and where you want to move to — your chosen culture. You can assess your current state by reviewing the moments that matter. When you articulate your chosen culture and develop your culture assets, be sure to include leaders' expectations. This allows you to tackle and align leader behaviours early on.

For organisations, reviewing and developing your current and chosen culture involves multiple people and

> Tackle and align leader behaviours early on.

can take time. As a leader considering your team's culture, you can accomplish this much faster.

A visible shift in leader behaviours and some quick wins in the moments that matter can kickstart your culture shift. Then it is a matter of working through the highest priority pain points or opportunities.

When you focus on the moments that matter, you prioritise your energy and efforts on those things that will have an outsized impact. Concentrate on gatherings, rituals, actions, symbols and stories (GRASS) as tangible areas where you can take action. (Re) designing the experience of moments that matter delivers shifts that are visible and felt by your team members. Multiply this effect by the behaviours leaders demonstrate and tolerate and you have the momentum to shift your culture.

This is the sprint phase, where you try to cover as much ground as possible before you run out of puff; the more momentum in the first few months, the more visible the shifts and the greater the belief of your teams. Shift as much as you can while you have the groundswell of energy, so that by the time you meet some hurdles, you have already delivered change. Otherwise, you risk running out of goodwill and stalling.

The relay team

I often reference the African proverb: 'If you want to go fast, go alone. If you want to go far, go together.' This applies to any change, particularly culture.

My track and field career was over by the time I turned 12, but I gravitated to cross-country. I've never really mastered the baton change of a relay. It was such a fraught experience each time I approached the handoff. I still remember hours of practising the baton exchange. Both runners keep moving forward, staying within their lanes and timing the handoff to occur in the zone. You can't pass too early, but you also can't take too long.

Culture shifts have a period when you transition from the initial sprint (where a smaller group does the heavy lifting) to the longer game. Often there is a lot of energy and focused attention during the sprint phase and the risk of losing it as you transition. So, like handing off a baton, be deliberate and plan the transition. Run in parallel for a period before you step back and let the team take it forward. Stay attentive and monitor how the team is going.

How will you know?

While I appreciate the need for garden variety success metrics, I have found the most impactful and rewarding change is the shift in the sentiment of team members and leaders. Cultures that work are full of happier people. It's easier to get stuff done. People enjoy their work more. And teams find joy in each other.

Of course, like all things in life, things change. Expectations shift. When you remove one barrier and climb the hill, you have a better view of the mountain beyond.

Culture is a moving target.

As the context you operate in changes, so too will the demands on your people and your culture. The necessary culture in an economic or industry downturn is resilient, focused, a bit grittier and grindier (made-up words, I know, but they work to describe this

> ## Culture is a moving target.

feeling). The necessary culture in a rapid growth phase is pacier, energised and a bit more forgiving. Mergers and acquisitions challenge and shift cultures in the lead up, during and beyond in the newly formed organisation.

Many boards and executives push for a culture dashboard. Investment in education to understand culture is important before implementing culture reporting. The metrics for culture are subjective and risk providing a false sense of security. Many an organisation with toxic culture has strong employee engagement scores reported.

Engagement is not culture. It is one indicator of culture but not the full picture.

The core engagement questions are known as say, stay and strive. While the wording of your questions may differ, generally we measure what you would say about your organisation (sometimes called pride or promoter), how much discretionary effort you put in (sometimes called motivation) and how long you intend to stay working (sometimes called commitment).

As mentioned in Chapter Two, self-reporting is often unreliable. The values and beliefs people say are important, for example, are often not reflected in how they actually behave (remember the IKEA anthropologists?). In the absence of any other metric, engagement scores will suffice as long as we understand that they are an indicator, not a measure.

Each organisation's set of measures will be different. One-size-fits-all will not support an organisational culture assessment of a unique culture. There are, however, some accepted measures to get you started. Some of these will be data constrained, but perhaps you could identify potential sources. As data and analytics evolve, further metrics will become available.[1] Consider the right mix of these measures of what matters most in your culture.

It's a marathon

Shifting culture is like running a marathon. It won't happen overnight. It takes time and gradual progress to reach your chosen culture. Just as you wouldn't do a handful of training runs and expect to complete 42 kilometres, a few people and a few changes to meetings won't create a team culture that works.

When it comes to shifting culture, it will not be smooth running. Nor will it be balanced. Culture shifts are a bit lumpier. Launches and events that inspire and excite are great to kickstart momentum and inject energy and engagement into a culture shift.

It will be hard. And it's not a matter of *if* the resistance will come, it's *when*.

But this is where the magic will happen. In a culture brimming with psychological safety, your people will step up and tell you where the problem is and as a team, together, you'll build a culture that works.

> # Lead a culture worth belonging to.

And over time, things will get better. You'll be a leader worth following, and you'll lead a culture worth belonging to. One that works for you. One that works for all your team (and your customers, stakeholders and community.)

Remember, culture is intangible, but it is actionable. And it is best shifted in the every day, by you as the leader of the team.

However, it is the shifts that occur in everyday work that result in more lasting change.

I hope that now you feel able to shift culture through everyday actions and are ready to lead culture as usual.

The Ground We've Covered

I could tell you a story about an incoming CEO who shifted a PowerPoint-mad culture to a Word culture in under 12 weeks by insisting he only read one-page documents. That might be in my next book...

#SOAP

#iykyk

In the meantime, here is this book on one page.

TL;DR

Culture matters more now than ever. Get clear. The challenge for leaders. Value culture. Investing in culture is worth it. Shift expectations.

What is culture anyway? Simplify culture. Define culture. Make culture actionable.

Shifting culture. Culture isn't somebody else's job. Culture is intangible but actionable. Build cultures that work. Everyday shifts.

Cultureshift formula. Your chosen culture. Multipliers. Moments that matter. Focus your efforts on what matters most.

GRASS. Shifting gears. A leader's role. Everyday actions. Some moments matter more.

Gatherings. Come together. Fix meetings. Act as the host (or guest). Drive for purpose, connection and contribution.

Rituals. Harness the power of rituals. Tap into emotion. Replace, refresh or design new rituals. Change your rituals, change your culture.

Actions. On purpose, with purpose. Consider context and consequences. Make it a habit. Take the OAR. Accountability matters.

Symbols. Offer clues to see your culture. Tap into unspoken communication. Symbols colour your culture. Leaders are symbols.

Stories. Culture is caught, not taught. Culture is shared through story. Stories are sticky. Share your own stories.

Hit the ground running. Get started. Lead your culture. Start today. Experiment and learn. It won't happen overnight, but it will happen.

The Green Room

Attribution matters

Over the last few decades, I have read widely and had thousands of conversations about culture. Where known, I have attributed concepts, research and quotes to the author. References are listed and linked wherever possible. Every effort has been made to trace (and seek permission for the use of) the original source of material used within this book. Where the attempt has been unsuccessful, I would be pleased to hear from the author or publisher to rectify any omission.

Fact, fiction or tall tale

The examples provided in the book are a mixture of lessons from observations or my own experience where I have led teams, coached and mentored leaders or consulted into organisations. They are naturally somewhat Australian-heavy, given the bulk of my career has been antipodean.

In some cases, I have named leaders and organisations where I think it is appropriate. In others, I have left it more generic for good reasons. This is not a book for critiquing the efforts of specific leaders or companies to shift their culture. Instead, it is a handbook for leaders to take everyday action.

If we've worked together, you may recognise the situation, the person or the organisation. You know who you are and what organisation you are part of, but it's not for me to share more. Perception is reality. My experience may not have been your experience. I have been, and continue to be, privy to many behind-door conversations and respect the trust and confidentiality of my clients and peers. However, each of these instances has happened and describes how I dealt with it. Nothing is made up. Nothing is theoretical.

Let's continue the conversation

Thank you for reading *Shift*.

Consider this an invitation to join me in a conversation about culture.

If you've found the book valuable, please share your story with me. I love hearing how leaders have put GRASS into action. There are as many variations of shifts as there are shades of green. You can email me directly at meredith@meredithwilson.com.au

I regularly share about culture on social media.

Join me on LinkedIn https://www.linkedin.com/in/meredithwilson/

Find me on Instagram https://www.instagram.com/meredith__wilson/

Meredith hosts a podcast for leaders, *Culture as Usual*, where she chats with leaders and experts about cultures that work. Listen wherever you find your favourite podcasts. You are invited to join my circle by visiting www.meredithwilson.com.au and subscribing. There you'll find more information about my programs and how we might work together.

If this book helped you, please share it with your friends, teammates and colleagues.

I look forward to continuing the conversation with you.

About the Author

Meredith is a culture strategist, speaker and executive mentor. She works with executives, CEOs and leadership teams to shape, shift, strengthen and lead cultures that work.

She makes culture simple and actionable.

After two decades of shaping, shifting, strengthening and leading organisational culture, Meredith knows what it takes in the real world. Her mission is to make culture less stuffy and fluffy and to share the tools of shifting culture. She can make culture work for you through her first-hand experience leading teams and culture through rapid growth, acquisitions, downturns, turnarounds and transformations in the corporate world.

Meredith has led many successful corporate transformations and turnarounds. She operated at executive and board levels for more than 15 years and led large teams globally and in ASX20 organisations through rapid growth and acquisitions, downturns, turnarounds and transformations across industries ranging from financial services to manufacturing and mining. She understands first-hand the competing demands for leaders, particularly the challenges of shifting culture in senior teams and mature organisations.

Her experience in the corporate world and deep knowledge of people and culture have made Meredith a highly sought-after speaker, executive coach and mentor. Unlike many coaches and consultants, her lived experience means she understands the challenges and opportunities. She is known for her pragmatic approach, creative solutions and deep knowledge of people and culture.

Meredith partners with executives, CEOs, founders and boards as an advisor, coach and mentor at critical moments, making an impact at the beginning of their tenure, chasing growth opportunities, or responding to tough operating environments, when culture matters most. She is their go-to when they want to lead a shift in their culture, build a cohesive senior team or shake up their organisation.

She has the experience, education, energy, intuition and imagination to help them lead in ambiguous conditions, navigate complex and evolving demands, and build readiness for the next normal and the never normal.

Meredith's experience is backed by extensive study and qualifications, with a Masters in Human Resources Management from Griffith University and degrees in Economics, History and German from the University of Queensland.

She is well regarded for her work with women in leadership roles in male-dominated industries and achieved industry recognition for reaching a 40% gender balance at every level of leadership at a large mining operation. This was remarkable given that when appointed, Meredith was the sole woman in the top three layers of the organisation.

Meredith co-authored the 2014 Queensland Male Champions of Change (QMCC) report *Changing the Game*.[1] She was a founding member of the Australian Veterans Employers Coalition (AVEC), which she chaired from 2018-2020, and she sat on the Prime Minister's Industry Advisory Council for Veteran Employment. Meredith is motivated to make a difference where arbitrary barriers to performance are cultural. Barriers that could be shifted to create opportunity.

Meredith is an inspiring, warm and engaging speaker and panellist. By sharing her personal experiences and real-life examples, she will have you laughing and learning about culture and leadership.

Acknowledgements

So, I have finally taken these ideas out of my head and written a book. It's an achievement I am incredibly proud of. Like anything worth achieving, it involved a tremendous support cast that inspired, encouraged and propelled me toward the finish line and beyond. Thank you.

To my family, who are my world. My husband, my partner, Wayne, whose unending love, encouragement and support sustain me, as did the daily desk deliveries of healthy lunches and snacks to keep me focused on writing. My son, Oscar, and daughter, Grace, have been my 'Why' through it all. My parents set me up for the path before me, including the forks and off-piste adventures, each in their own way. My brother and sister have kept it real. Thank you Kelly and Becca for carving out space, carrying the bags and helping me bring this book to life.

To the CHD crew, old and new, I value each and every text, hug, laugh, snapdragon and libertini (if you know, you know).

Thank you to my Thought Leaders compadres sharing the journey with me, shining the light on the path ahead and cheering along the winding road.

'*Grateful? Never enough*' for my mentors, Gad and Mel, and a host of leaders globally who continue to inspire me as they influence people to pay it forward.

To the many leaders and peers I have had the privilege of learning with and from, as we walked together through adventures around the world and closer to home. Many a late afternoon phone call or airport lounge conversation has contributed to my thinking on culture and leadership as it has evolved over the years.

Thanks to the leaders who backed me and invested heavily in initiatives to shift culture when I pitched a different approach.

Thank you to the clients, colleagues and connections who have partnered with me, responded to surveys and interviews, indulged my research, shared so transparently with me, allowed me to share their stories and agreed to be guests on my podcast.

To the teams I have had the pleasure of working with and the privilege to lead: thank you. We played big and learned a lot, creating team cultures where we could play to our strengths.

Further Reading

Chapter One: Culture Matters More Now Than Ever

Coaldrake, Peter. *Let the Sunshine In. Review of culture and accountability in the Queensland public sector.* Queensland Government, 2022. https://www.coaldrakereview.qld.gov.au/assets/custom/docs/coaldrake-review-final-report-28-june-2022.pdf

Grant Thornton, in collaboration with Oxford Economics. *Return on Culture: Proving the Connection between Culture and Profit.* Grant Thornton, 2019. https://www.oxfordeconomics.com/resource/return-on-culture-proving-the-connection-between-culture-and-profit/

Haynes, Kenneth. *Royal Commission into Misconduct in the Banking, Superannuation and Financial Services Industry Final Report.* Australian Government, 2019. https://www.royalcommission.gov.au/system/files/2020-09/fsrc-volume-1-final-report.pdf

Hinssen, Peter, and Misha Chellam. *The New Normal: Explore the limits of the digital world.* Mach Media, 2010.

Hinssen, Peter. *The Phoenix and the Unicorn. The Why, What and How of Corporate Innovation.* Peter Hinssen, 2020.

Oakes, Kevin. *Culture Renovation: 18 Leadership Actions to Build an Unshakeable Company.* 1st edition ed. McGraw Hill, 2021.

PwC. "PwC Global Culture Survey." PwC, 2018. https://www.strategyand.pwc.com/gx/en/insights/2018/global-culture-survey.html

PwC. "PwC Global Culture Survey". PwC, 2021. https://www.pwc.com/gx/en/issues/upskilling/global-culture-survey-2021.html

Rogers, Paul, Meehan, P. and Tanner, S. *Building a Winning Culture.* Bain & Company, 2006.

Chapter Two: What is Culture Anyway?

Crompvoets, Samantha. *Blood Lust, Trust & Blame (In The National Interest)*. Monash University Publishing, 2021.

Rothman, Joshua. *The Meaning of Culture*. The New Yorker, 2014. https://www.newyorker.com/books/joshua-rothman/meaning-culture

The Castle. Directed by Rob Sitch, Working Dog Productions, Roadshow Entertainment, 1997.

Chapter Three: Shifting Culture

Lewin, Kurt. "Frontiers in group dynamics: Concept, method and reality in social science; equilibrium and social change." *Human Relations*, vol. 1, no. 1, 1947.

Marquet, David. *Turn the Ship Around! A True Story of Turning Followers into Leaders*. Portfolio Publishing, 2013.

Schein, Edgar H. *Organisational Culture and Leadership*. Vol. 2. John Wiley & Sons, 2010.

Chapter Four: Cultureshift

Brown, Brené. *Atlas of the Heart: Mapping meaningful connection and the language of human experience*. Random House, 2021.

Pink, Daniel H. *Drive: The surprising truth about what motivates us*. Penguin, 2011.

Greene, Robert. *Mastery*. Penguin, 2013.

Chapter Five: GRASS

Schneider, Benjamin, and Karen M. Barbera (eds). *The Oxford Handbook of Organizational Climate and Culture*. Oxford Library of Psychology, Oxford Academic, 2014.

Chapter Six: Gatherings

Bluedorn, Allen C., Daniel B. Turban, and Mary Sue Love. "The effects of stand-up and sit-down meeting formats on meeting outcomes." *Journal of Applied Psychology*, vol. 84, no. 2, 1999.

Edmonson, Amy. *The Fearless Organisation: Creating Psychological Safety in the Workplace for Learning, Innovation and Growth.* John Wiley & Sons Inc., 2018.

Gunnarsson, Jan and Olle Blohm. *Hostmanship - The Art of Making People Feel Welcome.* Dialogos, 2013.

McKergow, Mark. *Host. Six New Roles of Engagement for Teams, Organisations, Communities, Movements.* Solutions Books, 2014.

Microsoft. "Managers Keep Teams Connected." *Microsoft Work Trend Index.* Microsoft, 2022. https://www.microsoft.com/en-us/worklab/work-trend-index/managers-keep-teams-connected

Microsoft. "Research Proves Your Brain Needs Breaks. New Options help you carve out downtime between meetings." *Work Trend Index Special Report.* Microsoft, April 2021. https://www.microsoft.com/en-us/worklab/work-trend-index/brain-research

Parker, Priya. *The Art of Gathering: How We Meet and Why it Matters.* Penguin, 2020.

Rogelberg, Steven G. *The Surprising Science of Meetings: How you can lead your team to peak performance.* Oxford University Press, 2018.

Chapter Seven: Rituals

Aaker, Jennifer, and Naomi Bagdonas. *Humor, Seriously: Why Humor Is a Secret Weapon in Business and Life (And how anyone can harness it. Even you.).* Currency, 2021.

Brooks, Alison Wood. "Research: Performing a Ritual Before a Stressful Task Improves Performance." *Harvard Business Review*, 2017. https://hbr.org/2017/01/research-performing-a-ritual-before-a-stressful-task-improves-performance

Brooks, Alison Wood, Juliana Schroeder, Jane L. Risen, Francesca Gino, Adam D. Galinsky, Michael I. Norton, and Maurice E. Schweitzer. "Don't stop believing: Rituals improve performance by decreasing anxiety." *Organisational Behaviour and Human Decision Processes*, vol. 137, 2016.

Grant, Heidi. "New Research: Rituals Make Us Value Things More." *Harvard*

Business Review, vol. 1, 2017. https://hbr.org/2017/01/new-research-rituals-make-us-value-things-more.

Kerr, James. *Legacy*. Hachette UK, 2013.

Keswin, Erica. *Rituals Roadmap: The Human Way to Transform Everyday Routines into Workplace Magic*. McGraw Hill Professional, 2021.

Keswin, Erica. "The Hidden Power of Workplace Rituals." *Harvard Business Review*, vol. 8, 2022. https://hbr.org/2022/08/the-hidden-power-of-workplace-rituals

Kniffin, Kevin M., Brian Wansink, Carol M. Devine, and Jeffery Sobal. "Eating together at the firehouse: How workplace commensality relates to the performance of firefighters." *Human Performance*, vol. 28, no. 4, 2015.

Watson-Jones, Rachel and Legare, Christine, "The Social Functions of Group Rituals", *Current Directions in Psychological Science*, vol. 25, no. 1, 2016.

Zak, Paul J. "The Neuroscience of Trust." *Harvard Business Review*, vol. 95, no. 1, 2017.

Chapter Eight: Actions

Clear, James. *Atomic Habits: An Easy & Proven Way to Build Good Habits & Break Bad Ones*. Avery, 2018.

Fogg, B.J. *Tiny Habits: The Small Changes That Change Everything*. Harvest, 2019.

Folkman, Joseph. *The Trifecta of Trust. The Proven Formula for Building and Restoring Trust*. River Grove Books, 2022.

Frankl, Viktor. *Man's Search for Meaning*. Edition 1 May 2011, 1946.

Hardy, Darren. *The Compound Effect. Jumpstart your income, your life, your success*. Darren Hardy, 2012.

Heffernan, Margaret. *Beyond Measure: The Big Impact of Small Changes*. Simon & Schuster, 2015.

Marquet, David. *Turn the Ship Around! A True Story of Turning Followers into Leaders*. Portfolio Publishing, 2013.

Marquet, David. *What is Leadership?* https://davidmarquet.com/my-story/

Olsen, Jeff. *The Slight Edge. Turning simple disciplines into massive success and happiness*. Greenleaf Publishing, 2013.

Pink, Daniel H. *When: The scientific secrets of perfect timing*. The Text Publishing Co., 2018.

Pink, Daniel H. *Drive: The surprising truth about what motivates us*. Penguin, 2011.

Chapter Nine: Symbols

Aurecon. *Aurecon launches visual employment contracts*. Aurecon, 2018. https://www.youtube.com/watch?v=zanKjKVqAsk

Beer, Jeff. "Why Ben & Jerry's fears Unilever wants to silence its progressive voice." *Fast Company*, August 2022. https://www.fastcompany.com/90780681/ben-jerrys-unilever-israel-west-bank-progressive-values

Coşar, B., Uzunçarşili, Ü., & Altindağ, E. "Do Not Neglect the Power of Symbols on Employee Performance: An Empirical Evidence from Turkey." *SAGE Open*, vol. 10, no. 4, 2020. https://doi.org/10.1177/2158244020967949

Higgins, James and Craig McAllaster. "If you want strategic change, don't forget to change your cultural artifacts." *Journal of Change Management*, vol 4, no. 1, 2004.

Chapter Ten: Stories

Aaker, Jennifer, and Naomi Bagdonas. *Humor, Seriously: Why Humor Is a Secret Weapon in Business and Life (And how anyone can harness it. Even you.)*. Currency, 2021.

Dolan, Gabrielle. *Stories for work: The essential guide to business storytelling*. John Wiley & Sons, 2017.

Goodwin, Doris Kearns. *Leadership: In Turbulent Times*. Simon & Schuster. 2019.

Naidu, Yamini. "Three Business Storytelling Secrets That No-one Tells You

About." *Yamini Naidu*, June 2018. https://yamininaidu.com.au/business-storytelling-techniques/3-business-storytelling-secrets-that-no-one-tells-you-about-2/

Naidu, Yamini. *Story Mastery: How leaders supercharge results with storytelling.* Yamini Naidu Consulting, 2019.

Naidu, Yamini. "Business Storytelling Permission. How to Nail it." *Yamini Naidu*, September 2020. https://yamininaidu.com.au/uncategorized/business-storytelling-permission-how-to-nail-it/

Snowden, D. *Narrative patterns*. Knowledge Management, ARK, 2001.

Chapter Eleven: Hitting the Ground Running

Corritore, M., Goldberg, A. and Srivastava, S. "The new analytics of culture." *Harvard Business Review*, vol. 1, 2020. https://hbr.org/2020/01/the-new-analytics-of-culture

Fried, Jason, and Heinemeier Hansson, David. *It Doesn't Have To Be Crazy at Work*. Harper Business, 2018.

Fried, Jason, and Heinemeier Hansson, David. *Remote: Office not Required*. Currency, 2013.

Fried, Jason, and Heinemeier Hansson, David. *Rework*. Currency, 2010.

Endnotes

Chapter One: Culture Matters More Now Than Ever

1. PwC. "PwC Global Culture Survey." PwC, 2021. https://www.pwc.com/gx/en/issues/upskilling/global-culture-survey-2021.html

2. PwC. "PwC Global Culture Survey." PwC, 2018. https://www.strategyand.pwc.com/gx/en/insights/2018/global-culture-survey.html

3. Oakes, Kevin. *Culture Renovation: 18 Leadership Actions to Build an Unshakeable Company*. McGraw Hill, 2021.

4. SC Johnson. https://www.scjohnson.com/en/about-us/the-johnson-family

5. Gallagher, Leigh. "Why Employees love staying at Marriott." *Fortune Magazine*, March 5, 2015. https://fortune.com/2015/03/05/employees-loyalty-marriott/

6. Arup, Sir Ove. "The Key Speech." Arup, 1970. https://www.arup.com/perspectives/publications/speeches-and-lectures/section/ove-arup-key-speech

7. Culture Amp. "What is a Culture First Company and why does it matter?" Culture Amp, 2016. https://www.youtube.com/watch?v=IAsBVB_89Us

8. Glassdoor. "Glassdoor Mission and Culture Survey." Glassdoor, 2019. https://www.glassdoor.com/about-us/app/uploads/sites/2/2019/07/Mission-Culture-Survey-Supplement.pdf

9. PwC. "PwC Global Culture Survey." PwC, 2021. https://www.pwc.com/gx/en/issues/upskilling/global-culture-survey-2021.html

10. Oakes, Kevin. *Culture Renovation: 18 Leadership Actions to Build an Unshakeable Company*. McGraw Hill, 2021.

11. Gallup. "How to build a better company culture." Gallup, 2022. https://www.gallup.com/workplace/327371/how-to-build-better-company-culture.aspx#ite-327398

12. Grant Thornton, in collaboration with Oxford Economics. "Return on Culture: Proving the Connection between Culture and Profit." Grant Thornton, 2019. https://www.oxfordeconomics.com/resource/return-on-culture-proving-the-connection-between-culture-and-profit/

13. Kay, Lisa. In conversation. April, 2022. https://www.linkedin.com/in/lisakay13/

14. Hinssen, Peter. *The Phoenix and the Unicorn. The Why, What and How of Corporate Innovation*. Peter Hinssen, 2020.

15. Grant Thornton, in collaboration with Oxford Economics. "Return on Culture: Proving the Connection between Culture and Profit." Grant Thornton, 2019. https://www.oxfordeconomics.com/resource/return-on-culture-proving-the-connection-between-culture-and-profit/

16. Microsoft. "Work Trend Index." *Microsoft Workplace Index*, 2021. https://www.microsoft.com/en-us/worklab/work-trend-index/

17. McKinsey. "Purpose: Shifting from why to how." McKinsey, 2020. https://www.mckinsey.com/capabilities/people-and-organizational-performance/our-insights/purpose-shifting-from-why-to-how

18. Haynes, Kenneth. *Royal Commission into Misconduct in the Banking, Superannuation and Financial Services Industry Final Report*, 2019. https://www.royalcommission.gov.au/system/files/2020-09/fsrc-volume-1-final-report.pdf

19. Coaldrake, Peter. *Let the Sunshine In. Review of culture and accountability in the Queensland public sector*, 2022. https://www.coaldrakereview.qld.gov.au/assets/custom/docs/coaldrake-review-final-report-28-june-2022.pdf

20. Grant Thornton, in collaboration with Oxford Economics. *Return on Culture: Proving the Connection between Culture and Profit*. Grant Thornton, 2019. https://www.oxfordeconomics.com/resource/return-on-culture-proving-the-connection-between-culture-and-profit/

21. Hagan, Alex. In conversation. November, 2022. https://www.alexhagan.co/

Chapter Two: What is Culture Anyway?

1. Lewin, Kurt. "Frontiers in group dynamics: Concept, method and reality in social science; equilibrium and social change." *Human Relations,* vol. 1, no. 1, 1947, pp.5–41.

2. Hall, Edward T. *Beyond Culture.* Double Day, 1976.

3. Gartner. *6 Key Gaps between Leader and Employee Sentiment on the Future Employee Experience.* Gartner, 2021. https://www.gartner.com/en/documents/4004102

4. Gartner. *6 Key Gaps between Leader and Employee Sentiment on the Future Employee Experience.* Gartner, 2021. https://www.gartner.com/en/documents/4004102

5. Heffernan, Margaret. *Beyond Measure: The Big Impact of Small Changes.* Simon & Schuster, 2015.

6. Crompvoets, Samantha. *Blood Lust, Trust & Blame (In The National Interest).* Monash University Publishing, 2021.

7. Morsley, Chris. In conversation. January, 2023. https://cmcglobal.com.au/

8. Hunter, Keana. In conversation. January, 2023. https://www.linkedin.com/in/keanahunter/

9. McAuley, Paul. In conversation. January, 2023. https://theindeliblelink.com/

10. Steel, Julia. In conversation. January, 2023. https://www.juliasteel.com/

11. French, David. In conversation. January, 2023. https://www.linkedin.com/in/davidfrench784/

12. Hoepper, Katherine. In conversation. January, 2023. https://www.linkedin.com/in/katherine-hoepper-b1b1123a/

13. Johnston, Lana. In conversation. January, 2023. https://www.linkedin.com/in/lanajohnston/

14. Kleine, Tara. In conversation. January, 2023. https://www.linkedin.com/in/tara-kleine-6a403946/

15. Webster, Karlie. In conversation. January, 2023.
    https://www.linkedin.com/in/karlie-webster-0b51541/

16. Staley, Alex. In conversation. January, 2023.
    https://www.linkedin.com/in/alexandra-staley-605b7336/

17. Hill, Tanya. In conversation. January, 2023.
    https://www.linkedin.com/in/tanya-hill-whs/

18. Matuszczak, Andrew. In conversation. January, 2023.
    https://www.linkedin.com/in/andrewmatuszczak/

19. Steele, Andrew. In conversation. January, 2023.
    https://www.linkedin.com/in/andrewdsteele/

20. Read, Aidan. In conversation. January, 2023.
    https://www.linkedin.com/in/aidanread/

21. Hobson-Powell, Anita. In conversation. January, 2023.
    https://www.linkedin.com/in/anitahobson-powel/

22. Reibel, Nathan. In conversation. January, 2023.
    https://www.linkedin.com/in/nathan-reibel-368a1726/

23. Rothman, Joshua. "The Meaning of 'Culture'." *The New Yorker*,
    December, 2014.
    https://www.newyorker.com/books/joshua-rothman/meaning-culture

24. *Oxford Dictionary of Philosophy*, edited by Simon Blackburn, 3rd ed.,
    Oxford University Press, 2023. https://www.oxfordreference.com/

25. *Oxford Dictionary of Philosophy*, edited by Simon Blackburn, 3rd ed.,
    Oxford University Press, 2023. https://www.oxfordreference.com/

26. *The Castle.* Directed by Rob Sitch. Working Dog Productions, Roadshow
    Entertainment, 1997.

27. Vaesen, Krist and Wybo Houkes. "Is human culture cumulative?"
    Current Anthropology, vol. 62, no. 2, 2021.

28. Churchill, Winston. "Those who do not learn from history are doomed
    to repeat it." *Speech to House of Commons*, British Houses of Parliament,
    1948.

29. Holmes, Oliver Wendell. *Holmes-Pollock Letters: The Correspondence of Mr Justice Holmes and Sir Frederick Pollock, 1874-1932*. 2nd ed., Bellknap Press: An Imprint of Harvard University Press, 1961.

Chapter Three: Shifting Culture

1. Robbins, Tony. "Where focus goes, energy flows. And where energy flows, whatever you're focusing on grows. In other words, your life is controlled by what you focus on. That's why you need to focus on where you want to go, not on what you fear." Twitter, June 14, 2022. https://twitter.com/TonyRobbins/status/1536370847555809281

2. *Everything Everywhere All At Once*. Directed by Kwan Daniel and Daniel Scheinert, IAC Films, 2022.

3. McKinsey. "Losing from Day One. Why even Successful Transformations fall short." *Insights*, McKinsey, 2021. https://www.mckinsey.com/~/media/mckinsey/business%20functions/people%20and%20organizational%20performance/our%20insights/successful%20transformations/december%202021%20losing%20from%20day%20one/losing-from-day-one-why-even-successful-transformations-fall-short-final.pdf

4. Emma Gibbens. In conversation. January, 2023. https://www.emmagibbens.com/

5. Google re: work. "Project Oxygen." *Re:Work*, Google, 2023. https://rework.withgoogle.com/blog/the-evolution-of-project-oxygen/

6. Clear, James. *Atomic Habits: An Easy & Proven Way to Build Good Habits & Break Bad Ones*. Avery, 2018.
Fogg, B.J. *Tiny Habits: The Small Changes That Change Everything*. Harvest, 2019.
Olsen, Jeff. *The Slight Edge*. Success Books, 2013.
Hardy, Darren. *The Compound Effect*. Darren Hardy, 2012.

7. Kelly, Paul and Kev Carmody. "From Little Things Big Things Grow." *Bloodlines*, 1991. https://www.youtube.com/watch?v=6_ndC07C2qw

8. Davis, Sarah. "New Year's Resolutions Statistics in 2023." *Forbes*, 11 Jan, 2023. https://www.forbes.com/health/mind/new-years-resolutions-statistics/#:~:text=The%20aforementioned%202020%20New%20Plate,lasting%20less%20than%20a%20month

9. Gibson, William. "the future is already here – it's just not evenly distributed." *The Economist*, 4 December, 2003.

Chapter Five: GRASS

1. Davies, Joel. Interview with Senior People Scientist, Dr Joel Davies, Culture Amp. January, 2023. https://www.cultureamp.com/contributors/joel-davies

2. Scholtes, Peter. *The Leader's Handbook: Making Things Happen, Getting Things Done.* McGraw-Hill. 1997.

3. Gino, Francesco. "The Business Case for Curiousity." *Harvard Business Review*, vol. 9, 2018. https://hbr.org/2018/09/the-business-case-for-curiosity

4. Dewey, John. *How We Think: A Restatement of the Relation of Reflective Thinking to the Educative Process.* D.C. Heath & Co Publishers, 1933.

5. Di Stefano, G., Gino, F., Pisano, G., & Staats, B. "Learning by thinking: How reflection improves performance" Accepted for publication on Management Science, *Harvard Business School NOM Unit Working Paper No. 14-093*, 2014. https://hbswk.hbs.edu/item/learning-by-thinking-how-reflection-improves-performance#:~:text=Reflecting%20on%20what%20has%20been,into%20higher%20rates%20of%20learning.

Chapter Six: Gatherings

1. McKergow, Mark. *Host. Six new roles of engagement for teams, organisations, communities, movements.* Solutions Books, 2014.

2. Parker, Priya. *The Art of Gathering: How we Meet and Why it Matters.* Penguin, 2020.

3. Pereira, Vijay. "Implementing No Meeting Days Improves Productivity." *HR Director Review*, May 2022. https://www.thehrdirector.com/features/hr-in-business/implementing-no-meeting-days-improves-productivity/

4. DeFilippis, Evan, Stephen Michael Impink, Madison Singell, Jeffrey T. Polzer, and Raffaella Sadun. "The impact of COVID-19 on digital communication patterns." *Humanities and Social Sciences Communications*, vol. 9, no. 1, 2022. https://www.nature.com/articles/s41599-022-01190-9

5. Rogelberg, Steven G. *The Surprising Science of Meetings: How you can lead your team to peak performance*. Oxford University Press, USA, 2018.

6. Microsoft. "Work Trend Index." *Microsoft Workplace Index*, 2021. https://www.microsoft.com/en-us/worklab/work-trend-index/

7. Rogelberg, Steven G. *The Surprising Science of Meetings: How you can lead your team to peak performance*. Oxford University Press, USA, 2018.

8. Parker, Priya. *The Art of Gathering: How we Meet and Why it Matters*. Penguin, 2020.

9. Ash, Bill. *Redesigning Conversations. A Guide To Communicating Effectively in the Family, Workplace, and Society*. Bill Ash, 2022.

10. Grant, Adam M. "There are 4 reasons to meet: to decide, learn, bond and do. If it doesn't serve one of those purposes, cancel it." Twitter, October 1, 2022. https://twitter.com/AdamMGrant

11. Bluedorn, Allen C., Daniel B. Turban, and Mary Sue Love. "The effects of stand-up and sit-down meeting formats on meeting outcomes." *Journal of Applied Psychology,* vol. 84, no. 2, 1999.

12. Sutton, Bob. "Why Big Teams Suck: Seven (Plus or Minus Two) is the Magical Number Once Again." *Work Matters*, 2014. https://bobsutton.typepad.com/my_weblog/2014/03/why-big-teams-suck-seven-plus-or-minus-two-is-the-magical-number-once-again.html

13. Whitefield, Bryan. *Risk Workshop Facilitation. The Art and Science of Facilitating Critical Conversations*. Bryan Whitefield, 2022.

14. Razzetti, Gustavo. *Remote Not Distant. Design a Company Culture that will help you thrive in a Hybrid Workplace*. Liberationist, 2022.

15. Burkus, David. *Leading From Anywhere: The Essential Guide to Managing Remote Teams*. Mariner, 2021.

16. Littlefield, Chad. 'Chad Littlefield: Make Connection Easy'. *YouTube*. https://www.youtube.com/channel/UCIZk6RPhfrjVQ4zGDNH2b9A

17. Brown, Brené. *Braving the Wilderness: The Quest for True Belonging and the Courage to Stand Alone*. Random House, 2017.

18. McKinsey. *It's not about the office, it's about belonging*. Insights, Mckinsey, 2022. https://www.mckinsey.com/capabilities/people-and-organizational-performance/our-insights/the-organization-blog/its-not-about-the-office-its-about-belonging

19. Yoshino, K. and Christie Smith. "Fear of Being Different Stifles Talent." *Harvard Business Review*, vol. 3, 2014. https://hbr.org/2014/03/fear-of-being-different-stifles-talent

20. Deloitte. "Creating a Culture of Belonging." *Human Capital Trends 2020*, Deloitte, 2020. https://www2.deloitte.com/us/en/insights/focus/human-capital-trends/2020/creating-a-culture-of-belonging.html

21. Edmonson, Amy. *The Fearless Organisation. Creating Psychological Safety in the Workplace for Learning, Innovation, and Growth*. Wiley, 2018.

22. Google re: work. "Understanding team effectiveness" *Re:Work*, Google, 2023. https://rework.withgoogle.com/guides/understanding-team-effectiveness/steps/introduction/

Chapter Seven: Rituals

1. Acknowledge This https://www.acknowledgethis.com.au/

2. Emma Gibbens. In conversation. January, 2023. https://www.emmagibbens.com/

3. Rhys Paddick. In conversation. January, 2023. https://www.rhyspaddick.com/

4. Aaker, Jennifer, and Naomi Bagdonas. *Humor, Seriously: Why Humor Is a Secret Weapon in Business and Life (And how anyone can harness it. Even you.)*. Currency, 2021.

5. Zak, Paul J. "The neuroscience of trust." *Harvard Business Review*, vol. 95, no.1, 2017.

6. Zak, Paul J. "The neuroscience of trust." *Harvard Business Review,* vol. 95, no.1, 2017.

7. Kniffin, Kevin, Wansink, Brian, Devine, Carol and Sobal, Jeffery. "Eating Together at the Firehouse: How Workplace Commensality Relates to the Performance of Firefighters." *Human Performance*, vol. 28, no.4, 2015.

8. Calne, Donald. *Within Reason: Rationality and Human Behavior*. Diane Pub Co, 1999.

9. Berkman, Elliot T. "The Neuroscience of Goals and Behaviour Change." *Consult Psychol Journal*, vol. 70, no.1, 2018.

10. McGrath, Rita. "Failing by Design." *Harvard Business Review*, vol. 4, 2011.

11. "What the heck is Arbejdsglaede?" Woohoo Inc. *What the heck is Arbejdsglaede*? https://www.whattheheckisarbejdsglaede.com/

12. Taylor, Adam. In conversation. December, 2022. https://www.linkedin.com/in/adametaylor1/

13. "Haka" New Zealand Tourism. *New Zealand*. https://www.newzealand.com/au/feature/haka/

14. Kerr, James. *Legacy*. Hachette UK, 2013.

15. Keswin, Erica, "The Hidden Power of Workplace Rituals." *Harvard Business Review*, 2022. https://hbr.org/2022/08/the-hidden-power-of-workplace-rituals

16. Watson-Jones, Rachel and Legare, Christine, '*The Social Functions of Group Rituals*', Current Directions in Psychological Science, vol 25(1), 2016.

17. Grant, Heidi. '*New Research: Rituals Make Us Value Things More.*', Harvard Business Review, vol. 1, 2017. https://hbr.org/2017/01/new-research-rituals-make-us-value-things-more.

18. Brooks, Alison Wood, Schroeder, Risen, Gino, Galinksy, Norton and Schweitzer, "Don't Stop Believing: Rituals Improve Performance by Decreasing Anxiety." *Organisational Behaviour and Human Decision Processes*, vol. 137, 2016.

19. Brooks, Alison Wood, "Research: Performing a Ritual Before a Stressful Task Improves Performance." Harvard Business Review, vol. 1, 2017. https://hbr.org/2017/01/research-performing-a-ritual-before-a-stressful-task-improves-performance.

20. Fogg, B.J. *Tiny Habits: The Small Changes That Change Everything.* Harvest, 2019.

Chapter Eight: Actions

1. Marquet, David. *Turn the Ship Around! A True Story of Turning Followers into Leaders.* Portfolio Publishing, 2013.

2. Grubbe, Deborah and DuPont. "Lessons from DuPont: How Culture, People, and Cost are Impacting your Safety Performance" *Health Care Delivery*, June, 2016.

3. Henderson, Michael. *Chiefing Your Tribe: How to Become a Leader Worth Following.* First Edition Limited, 2012.

4. Brosnan, Belinda. In conversation. May, 2023. https://www.belindabrosnan.com/

5. Folkman, Joseph. *The Trifecta of Trust. The Proven Formula for Building and Restoring Trust.* River Grove Books, 2022.

6. Frankl, Viktor. *Man's Search for Meaning.* Edition 1 May 2011, 1946.

7. Lowthorpe, Alan. In conversation. January, 2023. https://www.linkedin.com/in/alan-lowthorpe-6581651/

8. Avery, Christopher, Walker, Meri A., O'Murphy, E. *Teamwork Is an Individual Skill: Getting your work done when sharing responsibility.* Berrett-Koehler Publishers, 2001.

9. Crowley, Dermot. *Smart Work. Centralise, Organise, Realise. How to Boost your Productivity in 3 easy steps.* Wiley, 2016.

10. Newport, Cal. *Digital Minimalism: Choosing a Focused Life in a Noisy World.* Penguin, 2019.

11. Newport, Cal. *Deep Work: Rules for Focused Success in a Distracted World.* Piatkus, 2016.

12. Mead, Margaret. "Never doubt that a small group of thoughtful, committed citizens can change the world; indeed, it's the only thing that ever does." Attributed to American Anthropologist, Margaret Mead, by Douglas Keys in 1976.

13. Google re: work. "Understanding team effectiveness" *Re:Work*, Google, 2023. https://rework.withgoogle.com/guides/understanding-team-effectiveness/steps/introduction/

Chapter Nine: Symbols

1. Yunkaporta, Tyson. *Sand Talk: How Indigenous Thinking Can Save the World*. Harper One, 2021.

2. Aurecon. *Aurecon launches visual employment contracts* https://www.youtube.com/watch?v=zanKjKVqAsk

3. Aurecon Attributes https://www.aurecongroup.com/careers/culture/aurecon-attributes

4. Morgan, Jacob. *The Employee Experience Advantage: How to Win the War for Talent by Giving Employees the Workspaces they Want, the Tools they Need, and a Culture They Can Celebrate.* Wiley, 2017.

5. Marsden, Melissa. *The Next Workplace: Designing Dynamic Environments that Inspire Human Potential.* Comuniti, 2023.

6. *Hidden Figures*. Directed by Theodore Melfi. Twentieth Century Fox, 2016.

7. Ernst & Young. "Sustainability isn't what it used to be." *EY Future Consumer Index 2021*, Ernst & Young, 2021. https://www.ey.com/en_au/future-consumer-index/sustainability-isn-t-what-it-used-to-be
and
Gallup. "Environmental record factors for job seekers." *Gallup Poll Social Series: Environment*, Gallup, March 2021. https://news.gallup.com/poll/346619/environmental-record-factor-job-seekers.aspx

8. Brown, Brené. *Atlas of the Heart. Mapping meaningful connection and the language of human experience*. Penguin Random House. 2021.

9. PwC. "Creating Value Beyond the Deal: What if you took a different perspective to your M&A?" *Deals Report*, PWC, 2019. https://www.pwc.com/gx/en/services/deals/deals-report.html

10. PwC. "Creating Value Beyond the Deal: What if you took a different perspective to your M&A?" *Deals Report*, PWC, 2019. https://www.pwc.com/gx/en/services/deals/deals-report.html

11. Caliguiri, Paula. "When Unilever Bought Ben & Jerry's: A Story of CEO Adaptability." *Fast Company*, August, 2012. https://www.fastcompany.com/3000398/when-unilever-bought-ben-jerrys-story-ceo-adaptability

12. Higgins & McAllister. "If you want strategic change, don't forget to change your cultural artifacts." *Journal of Change Management*, vol. 4, no.1, 2004.

Chapter Ten: Stories

1. Goodwin, Doris Kearns. *Leadership: In Turbulent Times*. Simon & Schuster, 2019.

2. Stephens, Greg J., Lauren J. Silbert, and Uri Hasson. "Speaker–listener neural coupling underlies successful communication." *Proceedings of the National Academy of Sciences*, vol. 107, no. 32, 2010.

3. Wiessner, Polly W. "Embers of society: Firelight talk among the Ju/'hoansi Bushmen." *Proceedings of the National Academy of Sciences*, vol. 111, no.39, 2014.

4. Wiessner, Polly W. "Embers of society: Firelight talk among the Ju/'hoansi Bushmen." *Proceedings of the National Academy of Sciences*, vol. 111, no.39, 2014.

5. Wiessner, Polly W. "Embers of society: Firelight talk among the Ju/'hoansi Bushmen." *Proceedings of the National Academy of Sciences*, vol. 111, no.39, 2014.

6. Twynham, Brad. In conversation. February, 2023. https://www.bradtwynham.com/

7. Yunkaporta, Tyson. *Sand Talk: How Indigenous Thinking Can Save the World*. Harper One, 2021.

8. Gregory, Dan. In conversation. January, 2023. https://tbr.news/dan-gregory

9. Routledge, Clay. "The surprising power of nostalgia at work." *Harvard Business Review*, vol. 4, 2021. https://hbr.org/2021/04/the-surprising-power-of-nostalgia-at-work

10. Terry, Penny. In conversation. January, 2023. http://pennyterry.com/

11. Husband, Jon. "What is Wirearchy?" *Wirearchy*, 2013. http://wirearchy.com/what-is-wirearchy/

12. Husband, Jon. "What is Wirearchy?" *Wirearchy*, 2013. http://wirearchy.com/what-is-wirearchy/

13. Dolan, Gabrielle. *Stories for work: The essential guide to business storytelling*. John Wiley & Sons, 2017.

14. Dolan, Gabrielle. *Stories for work: The essential guide to business storytelling*. John Wiley & Sons, 2017.

15. DiBella, Gianna. In conversation. January, 2023. https://www.linkedin.com/in/gianna-di-bella-6a4a2a129

16. Downer Professional Services https://www.downerprofessionalservices.com.au/

17. Callahan, Shawn. *Putting Stories to Work*. Pepperberg Press, 2016.

18. Thompson, Jason. In conversation. May, 2023. https://www.jasonthompson.ca/

19. Terry, Penny. In conversation. January, 2023. http://pennyterry.com/

20. *Oprah Winfrey receives the Cecil B. DeMille Award*, Golden Globes, Youtube, 2018. https://www.youtube.com/watch?v=LyBims8OkSY

21. Blanco, Richard. *How to love a Country: Poems*. Beacon Press, 2019.

22. Adam Grant. "The 4 deadly sins of work culture." *Work-life with Adam Grant*, season 5, 2022. https://adamgrant.net/podcasts/work-life/

Chapter Eleven: Hitting the Ground Running

1. Corritore, M., Goldberg, A. and Srivastava, S. "The new analytics of culture." *Harvard Business Review*, vol.1, 2020. https://hbr.org/2020/01/the-new-analytics-of-culture

About the Author

1. Wilson, Meredith and Morgan, Lisa. *Changing the Game*, Queensland Male Champions of Change (QMCC), 2014.

www.ingramcontent.com/pod-product-compliance
Lightning Source LLC
Chambersburg PA
CBHW071340210326
41597CB00015B/1513